The Wit & Wisdom of Benjamin Franklin

The Wit & Wisdom of
Benjamin Franklin

James C. Humes

Foreword by David Eisenhower

Gramercy Books
New York

To Thacher Longstreth;
Who is the closest thing to "Mr. Philadelphia"
since Benjamin Franklin

Copyright © 1995 by James C. Humes

All rights reserved under International and Pan-American Copyright Conventions.

This 2001 edition is published by Gramercy Books, an imprint of Random House Value Publishing, a division of Random House, Inc., New York, by arrangement with HarperCollins Publishers.

Gramercy is a registered trademark and the colophon is a trademark of Random House, Inc.

Random House
New York • Toronto • London • Sydney • Auckland
www.randomhouse.com

Designed by Barbara DuPree Knowles

Printed in the United States of America

Library of Congress Cataloging-in-Publication Data

Humes, James C.
    The wit & wisdom of Benjamin Franklin / James C. Humes ; foreword by David Eisenhower.
        p. cm.
    Originally published: New York : HarperCollins, c1995
    Includes bibliographical references (p.) and index.
    ISBN 0-517-16345-4
    1. Franklin, Benjamin, 1706–1790—Quotations. 2. Quotations, American. I. Title: Wit and wisdom of Benjamin Franklin.   II. Title

E302.6F8   A25 2001
973.3'092—dc21
                                                                00-052832

8 7 6 5 4 3

Contents

Acknowledgments

Any recital of appreciation must begin with one of the greatest autobiographies ever written. Two centuries later *The Autobiography of Benjamin Franklin* reads easily. His simple style is unencumbered by the ornate language of so many eighteenth-century writers.

Carl Van Doren's *Benjamin Franklin* is the standard authoritative biography, but I followed Whitfield Bell's advice that James Parton's two-volume *Benjamin Franklin* is the most complete portrait of America's most lovable historical personality. Dr. Bell's eighteen volumes of Franklin's papers is a massive work of scholarship to peruse, but worth the effort.

I am grateful to Roy Goodman, director of the American Philosophical Society, who was generous in his time and advice. The society, which Franklin established, is America's most venerable scholarly society and is esteemed throughout the world. Two books that Roy Goodman suggested were Paul Ford's *The Many-sided Franklin* and especially Paul Maxwell Zall's *Ben Franklin Laughing,* both of which I found to be rich sources.

The book that offers the most entertaining portrait of the colorful Franklin is Seymour Block's *Benjamin Franklin—His Wit, Wisdom and Women.*

An institution any lover of Franklin will want to visit is the Franklin Institute. They were most helpful in finding for me Franklin's proposed alphabet and particularly the new letters he devised.

On a different note I thank the Murray Opticians in Chestnut Hill, Philadelphia—Joseph W. Cooney, Joseph S. Cooney, and Walter Scarborough—who for years have loaned me Benjamin Franklin spectacles for my one-man show "What's Happening at the Convention, Dr. Franklin?"

An additional note of appreciation goes to Richard A. Eisenbeis, who gave me a tip on Bushnell and the submarine. Richard is the son of an old childhood friend, Dr. Richard Eisenbeis.

As in my *Wit & Wisdom of Winston Churchill,* this book in its finished form owes much to the probing queries of my editor, Stephanie Gunning.

Joan Hendrix, who oversees the library of the Union League in Philadelphia among her other curatorial duties, deserves praise for her patience and assistance.

Nancy Kowalchik, my typist, despite my messy handwriting, did a thoroughly professional job in the various revisions.

Finally, I am indebted to David Eisenhower for writing the Foreword to this book, which is a sequel to *The Wit & Wisdom of Winston Churchill,* whose Foreword was written by the late President Nixon, David's father-in-law. My wife, Dianne, and I treasure our association and friendship over the years with both the Nixon and Eisenhower families.

Foreword

Benjamin Franklin has always been one of my favorite personalities in history. That is not surprising, considering that I am a Pennsylvanian and have taught politics at the University of Pennsylvania, which Franklin established.

Franklin, however, was not born in Pennsylvania, but in Massachusetts. It has been said—not by me—that the two greatest Pennsylvanians were not natives but rather ones who chose to adopt this Commonwealth as their state: Benjamin Franklin, who moved from Boston to live in Philadelphia, and Dwight David Eisenhower of Kansas, who would make his home in Gettysburg. It is hard for me to argue with that assertion.

James Humes's book *The Wit & Wisdom of Benjamin Franklin*—especially in his sections "Franklin Firsts," "Inventions, Ideas, and Discoveries" and "Renaissance Roles"—dramatically evinces the incredible range of Franklin's creativity and genius.

But what particularly fascinated me about his book were some of the parallels between Franklin's life and that of my grandfather. Even if more than a couple of centuries separated their careers, the two shared a talent for projecting their "down-home Americanism" into winning friends and shaping policy not only in councils of government here but also abroad.

No other Americans were so lionized in Europe as Benjamin Franklin and Dwight Eisenhower. That attribute of character that makes others admire, trust, and believe in them may be partially innate, but it is also acquired. Both men had their share of ego but, as a matter of discipline, they controlled it while cultivating the habit of listening and letting others do the talking.

To read the first section on "Sage Sayings"—in so many of which Franklin urged the virtues of reticence, modesty, and prudence and counseled against the taking of credit and the spreading of gossip—is to remember some of my grandfather's rules. He always said, "Do not engage in personalities." Like Franklin, the letters Eisenhower often drafted in hot temper he never sent.

I was struck by Thomas Jefferson's observation that he never heard Franklin directly contradict another in a discussion. General Eisenhower had strong opinions but, like Franklin, he never browbeat or bullied those with divergent views. Franklin and Eisenhower instead were deft in nurturing the common areas of agreement and then maneuvering the discussion into a common consensus.

Both arrived in France with a fame that invited idolatry—Franklin as the scientist and author and Eisenhower as the D-Day liberator and general. Such phenomenal popularity was money in the bank, but neither of them squandered it by arrogance of rank or pretensions of vanity. On the contrary, they remained the simple and unaffected Americans who first captured the hearts of Europeans.

In the modern language of public relations, we might say that Minister Franklin made a statement when he wore no wig and shunned the velvet and silk fineries in favor of American homespun in his first appearance at the court of Versailles. Two centuries later, Eisenhower cultivated the role of "the G.I. general" who was nicknamed "Ike."

Ambition spurred the rise of both men from humble beginnings, but they were careful not to let their ambition show. They both shared a distaste for the pompous struttings of the vainglorious. Franklin was not fond of John Adams and Eisenhower was no admirer of MacArthur, but both Franklin and Eisenhower could submerge their feelings to work with those they disliked.

Franklin and Eisenhower manifested disdain for the professional politician, yet both mastered the art of politics. They were not unaware of how their public postures of genial humility would enhance their appeal to the nobility of England and France. Franklin always introduced himself, "I'm Benjamin Franklin, a printer." Eisenhower liked to describe himself to the elite of Europe as "a simple soldier." The modesty of their demeanor masked the complexities of shrewd practitioners of statecraft.

If there are parallels to be drawn from their careers, the personalities of the two were disparate. Franklin had a playful side that lent itself to spoofs and put-ons, which the professional soldier Eisenhower did not indulge in.

In some ways it could be said that the contemporary leader that Franklin most evokes is Churchill. Both were Renaissance men. Churchill was a soldier, journalist, author, historian, parliamentarian, artist, and bricklayer. The printer Franklin played the roles of editor, author, legislator, scientist, inventor, diplomat, and Founding Father. Both were endowed with a creative genius—a talent that did not burn itself out quickly but raged on productively decade after decade.

Then, too, both Churchill and Franklin shared an impish wit. A "little boy naughtiness" was always part of their charm.

Still, in his sense of humor and penchant for storytelling, Franklin was the forerunner of Abraham Lincoln. Both were natural raconteurs who could spin funny anecdotes and concoct parables to delineate problems and issues. Ever since frontier life, storytelling has developed as an American art form and the quintessential examples are Franklin and Lincoln.

It has been said that my grandfather could manifest a boyish grin that looked as if it was Huck Finn painted by Norman Rockwell. Franklin also had a sunny, benign face that personified the homespun American whose eminence defied the European notions of class. The plain printer and simple soldier—despite the public protestations to the contrary—were adroit politicians with skill in the diplomat's art of persuasion.

David Eisenhower

Preamble

In 1777, Benjamin Franklin resigned as the U.S. minister to France in order to return to Philadelphia. Months later, Thomas Jefferson, the new American envoy, was met in Versailles by Count Vergennes, the French prime minister.

Vergennes said, "Monsieur Jefferson, have you come to replace Dr. Franklin?"

Jefferson answered, "No one could ever replace Benjamin Franklin, I am only succeeding him."

I have sometimes almost wished it had been my destiny to be born two or three centuries hence.

—BENJAMIN FRANKLIN, 1788

Introduction

Benjamin Franklin first became a subject of study for me ten years ago. It was as if fate had taken my hand.

I was addressing a political audience of over two hundred at a hotel breakfast in Wilkes-Barre, Pennsylvania. Just before I was to mount the dais, a handsome older woman—looking younger than her seventy-odd years—approached me. Before she could introduce herself, I had a sense of recognition. She was Jane Hammer Muffley and had been my father's secretary; my last memory of seeing her was at his funeral. My father had been a judge of a neighboring county and had died in January 1943.

Her once gold hair had turned to white, but the clean chiseled lines of her face struck an immediate response. She said, "James, I brought to you the items on your father's desk the way he left it that night he went to address that PTA group at the school."

My father, whom I resemble, suffered a cerebral stroke while digging his car out of a snowbank near the school whose audience he never was to address.

There in that hotel banquet hall she handed me a desk blotter, the calendar opened to the day of his death with the speech time noted: "8:00 PM Sheridan School P.T.A." Along with that she handed me a book that was a collection of Franklin's works with the pages opened to Franklin's talk at the close of the Constitutional Convention. Paragraphs had been underlined by my father in red pencil.

Only one who has lost a father at an early age (I was eight) will fully understand a son's compulsion to know everything about the man whom he never really got to know. This need was particularly keen in me because my father was a revered public figure about whom I would hear—even a half century later—almost mythic tales of his compassion and his personal kindnesses to people.

So after my talk that night in Wilkes-Barre I read through Franklin's collected works, which included his autobiography, and I immediately felt an affinity with his life.

Like Franklin, I had arrived in Philadelphia as a young man. He served in the Pennsylvania General Assembly, as did I. During the Revolution, Franklin was America's first diplomat. I also had been a diplomat—serving in the U.S. Department of State and representing our country in various missions abroad. After George Washington was sworn in as our first chief executive, Franklin was a source of presidential counsel. I was a speechwriter in the White House.

Stretching the comparison, I could also liken myself to Franklin by citing my career of writing. Furthermore, he founded the University of Pennsylvania, where I teach.

Career similarities are one thing—genius is another. Few if any in American history approach the multifaceted brilliance of Benjamin Franklin. Yet I do share with him at least one of his predilections or traits: collecting quotations and anecdotes, such as the ones found in this book.

Franklin tells us to read books with a notebook alongside so that we can jot down lines that capture our fancy or describe our own thoughts. A collection of anecdotes is the arsenal of any speaker in demand. But the key to speaking success is the anecdote that enlivens a point and entertains the audience.

Franklin was a collector of stories. Be it by fable or parable, Franklin would teach, educate, and explain. He was the first in a long line of celebrated Americans who was a raconteur.

If I find something of myself in Benjamin Franklin, I am far from unique. The small-town businessman who heads the Rotary Club, the hobbyist who likes to tinker in his cellar workshop, the community volunteer who gives his time as a township fireman, the small-city newspaper editor who hustles each night to meet the morning deadline, the shopkeeper who worries over rising costs, the good citizen who heads up the local hospital drive—all of these are Ben Franklins, in a sense. Just about everybody can identify with at least one facet of Franklin.

Benjamin Franklin established many firsts on this side of the Atlantic. He was our first scientist, first inventor, first philanthropist, first postmaster, first diplomat. But more than that, he was the first American.

When George Washington was still mastering surveying, when

John Adams was entering Harvard, when Thomas Jefferson was taking his first steps, Benjamin Franklin was calling himself an American. He was the first colonial leader to do so at a time when others identified themselves as a Pennsylvanian, Virginian, or Massachusetts man. Perhaps it was because as colonial postmaster general Franklin was the first to traverse and visit all the thirteen colonies.

Washington and Jefferson were eighteenth-century English country squires and John Adams could easily have been a London barrister of that era. Yet Franklin had advantage neither of birth nor of education. He was the first American rags-to-riches success story, a century and a half before the name Horatio Alger ever appeared in print. Franklin was the first to believe in the American dream—possibly because he saw it come true in his own life.

There is no monument in our capital city to Benjamin Franklin, as there is to George Washington. Nor are his contributions recognized by a memorial, as are those of both Thomas Jefferson and Abraham Lincoln. It might be argued that the spirit of Franklin is sensed in Independence Hall in Philadelphia, which was the old State House where Franklin had served as clerk of the House, legislator, and member of the Second Continental Congress, which declared the Resolves of Independence. Later the hall housed the proceedings of the Constitutional Convention, which Franklin attended as its oldest delegate. Independence Hall, however, is first and foremost a testament to the birth of America, even if for a half century Franklin was the most famous face found there.

Yet though Franklin has no official monument or memorial in his name, he is, arguably, the greatest American. Certainly in his day he was recognized not just as the greatest American, but as the greatest man in the world. Universities both in America and abroad showered degrees and honors on him; Josiah Wedgwood's cameo likeness of him was the fastest-selling memento in Britain and in Europe. The world saw in the unschooled and plainly dressed Franklin the raw promise of the New World and the uniqueness of America.

Sage Sayings

Benjamin Franklin is the most quoted American. Often we repeat his maxims without remembering the source: "God helps those who help themselves," "Time is money," and "Fish and houseguests stink after three days," not to mention "Early to bed, early to rise, makes a man healthy, wealthy and wise."

Most of his adages came from the mouth of Poor Richard in the *Poor Richard's Almanack,* which Franklin published. Richard Saunders, a comic invention of Franklin, was a Quaker astronomer who, readers thought, was the source of the seasonal forecasts that were the staple of the almanac. By such a ruse, Franklin insulated himself from the criticism of those who blame the weatherman for bad weather.

Franklin salted the farmers' fare with homely aphorisms. Many he dusted off from ancient sources and reburnished with his own sander for the American colloquial ear. Among those he plagiarized were the English authors Francis Bacon, John Ray, and John Selden and the French pundits Montaigne, Rabelais, and François de la Rochefoucald.

La Rochefoucald said, "The greatest monarch on the greatest throne is obliged to sit on his own ass." Under Franklin's alchemy it became, "No matter how high the throne, he still sits on his own ass."

Seldes's line "A man in a passion rides a horse that runs away with him" was shortened to "A man in passion rides a mad horse."

Even the name "Poor Richard" was partly borrowed. *Poor Robin* was the name of a seventeenth-century English almanac.

Sometimes the versifier in Franklin took hold of his pen:

Great estates may venture more
Little boats keep close to shore

Franklin may have inherited his rhyming ear from his mother's kin. Both his grandfather and uncle on his mother's side were amateur poets. Franklin, though, entertained no poetic pretensions. He wrote:

I know as well as thee that I am no poet born
It is a trade, I never learnt nor indeed could learn
If I make verses — tis in spite
Of nature and my stars I write

Franklin loved the ring of rhyme. With the flair of a born advertising man, he sensed that the more comic and corny the verse was, the longer it would echo in the reader's ear. It is not surprising that Ben the sloganeer became the Ben the balladeer—one of the most prolific songwriters in colonial America. But it is the sayings of Poor Richard that won for Franklin the sobriquet "Sage of America," not just in his homeland but—even in his day—throughout Europe and the world.

Of course, many of the quotations cited in this work come from sources other than the almanac, such as his autobiography, his essays, and his voluminous correspondence.

Yet Franklin's fame as a maxim maker is owed to Poor Richard. His aphorisms on work, thrift, and self-denial may sound quaint today in a time of credit card binges, savings-and-loan failures, and billion-dollar national debt. Yet curiously the criticism of Franklin in this century came not so much from the materialists as from the Marxists, who ridiculed Franklin's recipes for success. In the 1930s some academics and writers from the left called him "without soul," and others termed him "the piggy-bank pundit," "the boss's flack," and "an apologist for the Protestant ethic."

Though hardly a leftist, Mark Twain had a point when he echoed the complaints of all boys who heard the words of Franklin in scoldings by their father. Franklin, who had a lot of Tom Sawyer in him, I think, would have agreed with Tom's creator.

Franklin didn't like prigs. He preferred "speckled characters." In fact, it was to escape the pious Puritans that he came to Philadelphia. Yet he knew the market he was trying to reach—the stolid Pennsylvania farmers who would take to heart these maxims of self-reliance and thrift.

These are scraps from the table of wisdom that if well digested, yield strong nourishment to thy mind.

—Franklin on an edition of *Poor Richard's Almanack*

ża ża ża

ACTIVITY

☞ It seems my fate constantly to wish for repose and never to obtain it.

ADMINISTRATION

☞ A little neglect may breed mischief; for want of a nail, a shoe was lost; for want of a shoe, the horse was lost; and for want of a horse, the rider was lost.

ADULATION

☞ Admiration is the daughter of ignorance.

ADVICE

☞ A word to the wise is enough; and many words won't fill a bushel.

☞ They that won't be counseled, can't be helped.

☞ In the multitude of counselors, there is safety.

☞ We can give advice but we cannot give conduct.

AGRICULTURE

☞ Agriculture will [in the future] diminish its labor and double its productivity.

ALCOHOL

☞ There are more old drunkards than old doctors.

☞ Drink water, put the money in your pocket, and leave the day bellyache [hangover] in the punch bowl.

There can't be good living where there is not good drinking.

ALLY

The weakest foe boasts some revenging power —
the weakest friend some serviceable hour.

ALTRUISM

Great good nature, without prudence, is a great misfortune.

AMBITION

Nothing humbler than ambition when it is about to climb.

That laudable ambition is too commonly misapplied and often ill-employed.

AMERICA

Establishing the liberties of America will not only make that people happy, but will have some effect in diminishing the misery of those who in other parts of the world groan under despotism by rendering it more circumspect and inducing it to govern with a lighter hand.

When foreigners after looking about for some other country in which they obtain more happiness, give a preference to ours, it is proof of attachment which ought to excite our confidence and affection.

By the next century the population will be more than the people of England and the greatest number of Englishmen will be on this side of the Atlantic.

❧ America, an immense territory, favored by Nature with all advantages of climate, soils, great navigable rivers and lakes must become a great country populous and mighty, and will in less time than is generally conceived, shake off any shackles imposed upon her.

❧ I know too well the badness of our general taste.

AMERICAN
❧ Every man in America is employed—an idle man here is a disgrace.

❧ In America, they do not inquire of a stranger, "What is he?" but, "What can he do?"

❧ God will finish his work and establish freedom and lovers of liberty will flock from all parts of Europe with their fortunes to participate with us in that freedom.

ANCESTORS
❧ I have ever had pleasure in obtaining any little anecdotes of my ancestors.

❧ There is no pride like pride of ancestry.

❧ A man who makes boast of his ancestors doth but advertise his own insignificance, for the pedigrees of great men are commonly known.

ANGER
❧ What's begun in anger, ends in shame.

చ He that can compose himself is wiser than he that composes books.

చ A man in a passion rides a mad horse.

చ Avoid extremes—forbear resenting injuries so much as you think they deserve.

APPLE
చ An apple a day keeps the doctor away.

ARBITRARINESS
చ The language of the [British] proposal is this: try on my fetters first and then if you don't like them, petition and we will consider [removing them].[1]

ARGUMENT
చ Shun party-wrangling, mix not in debate with bigots in religion or the state [party politics].

ARGUMENTATIVE
చ People of good sense, I have since observed, seldom fall into disputation, except lawyers and university men.

చ Better is a little with content than much with contention.

చ For of all things—I hate altercation.

---

[1] Franklin was explaining his objection to the British tax policy in 1770.

∽ It is a bad temper of mind that takes delight in opposition.

ARMY
∽ An army is a devouring monster, and when you have raised it, you have in order to subsist it—not only the charges of pay, clothing, provisions, arms, and ammunition but also the contingent and additional knavish charges of numerous tribes of contractors to defray—with those of every other dealer who furnishes articles wanted for your army and then takes advantage of that want to demand exorbitant prices.

ARTS
∽ The arts have always traveled westward.[2]

BANALITY
∽ There are lazy minds as well as lazy bodies.

BEHAVIOR
∽ It is never too late to mend.

BETRAYAL
∽ *He for a post or base sordid pelf*
His country betrays, makes a rope for himself.

BOOKS
∽ Read much but not too many books.

---

[2] A letter to artist Charles Wilson Peale.

☙ I sat up in my room reading the greatest part of the night, when the book was borrowed in the evening and to be returned early in the morning lest it should be missed or wanted.

☙ When I was young and had time to read, I had no books. Now that I am old and have the books, I have no time to read.

☙ Reading makes a full man, meditation a profound man, discourse a clear man.

☙ I would advise you to read with a pen in your hand and enter in a little book short hints of what you feel that is common or that may be useful; for this will be the best method of imprinting such portcullis in your memory.

☙ From a child I was fond of reading and all the little money that came in my hands was ever laid out in books.

☙ Good books of all sorts may employ your leisure and enrich you with treasures more valuable than those which you might have procured in your usual vocations.

☙ *Some books we read, tho' few there are that hit*
   The happy point where wisdom joins with wit.

BORROWING
☙ He that goes a-borrowing, goes a-sorrowing.

*   *   *

BRIBERY

ℤ We could have purchased our independence at one-tenth the cost of defending it.[3]

BRITAIN

ℤ I was fond to a folly of our British connections and it was with infinite regret that I saw the necessity you would force us into of breaking it.

ℤ Give me leave, Master John Bull, to remind you that you are *related to all mankind* and therefore it less becomes you than anybody, to affront and abuse other nations. But you have mixed with your many virtues, a pride, a haughtiness and insolent contempt for all but yourself that I am afraid will, if not abated, procure you one day or other a handsome drubbing.

ℤ You are a Member of Parliament and one of that majority which has doomed my country to destruction. You have begun to burn our towns and murder our people. Look upon your hands! They are stained with the blood of your relations. You and I were long friends, you are now my enemy and I am yours.[4]

BUILDINGS

ℤ Building is an old man's amusement. The advantage is for his posterity.

---

[3] Franklin was referring to the bribing of British members of Parliament.

[4] Franklin is writing to his English friend William Strahan.

BUREAUCRACY

☞ Business is best managed and to most advantage by those who are immediately interested in the profit of it and that the Trading Companies [state-run companies or corporations] are generally more profitable to the servants [bureaucrats] of the company than to the proprietors or the public.

BUREAUCRATS

☞ You who are a thorough courtier see everything through government eyes. [5]

☞ I doubt their sincerity even in the political principle they profess and deem them mere time-servers seeking their own political emoluments.

CAPITAL PUNISHMENT

☞ I think it right that the issue of murder should be punished with death not only as an equal punishment of the crime but also to prevent other murders.

CAPITALISM

☞ Is not the hope of one day being able to purchase and enjoy luxuries a great spur to labor and industry?

CASH

☞ There are three faithful friends: an old wife, an old dog, and ready money.

---

[5] Franklin is writing to his son William, who had been appointed the Royal Governor of New Jersey.

CHALLENGE

‟ We may make these times better, if we bestir ourselves.

CHANGE

‟ Discontented minds and fevers of the body are not to be cured by changing beds or businesses.

‟ Can anything be constant in a world which is eternally changing?

CHARACTER

‟ *Some grow mad by studying much to know*
But who grows mad by studying good to grow.

‟ Show thyself a man.

‟ There was never yet a great man that was not at the same time truly virtuous.

CHARITY

‟ He that lives on hope, dies fasting.[6]

‟ Faith, Hope, and Charity have been called the three steps of Jacob's ladder, reaching from earth to heaven. Faith is the ground floor, Hope is one part of stairs . . . the best room in the house at the top is Charity.

---

[6] The original version said, "He that lives on hope, dies farting."

CHARM

∽ As charms are nonsense, so nonsense is charm.

CHEATING

∽ He'll cheat without scruple who can without fear [of being caught].

CHESS

∽ By playing chess we may learn foresight, circumspection, caution, and patience.

CHILDREN

∽ Love well and whip well.

∽ *Let thy child's first lesson be obedience*
  and the second will be what thou wilt.

CHRISTIANITY

∽ He who shall introduce into public affairs the principles of primitive Christianity shall revolutionize the world.

CHRISTMAS

∽ How many observe Christ's birthday; how few His precepts! O 'tis easier to keep a Holiday, than Commandments!

CHURCH

∽ The bell calls others to church, but itself never minds the sermon.

CHURCH AND STATE

✍ When religion is good, it will support itself, but when it cannot support itself and God does not take care to support it so that its professors are obliged to call for the help of a civil power, it's a sign, I apprehend, of a bad one.

CIVIL RIGHTS

✍ Those who have no voice nor vote in the electing of representatives, do not enjoy liberty but are absolutely enslaved to those who have votes.

CLEANLINESS

✍ Tolerate no uncleanliness in body, clothes, or habitation.

"COFFEE-TABLE BOOKS"

✍ You have a law, I think, against butchers blowing veal to make it look fatter. Why not one against booksellers blowing books to make them look bigger?

COLONIALISM

✍ Every man in England seems to consider himself as a piece of sovereign over America.

COLONIES

✍ It is a common, but mistaken notice here [in England] that the Colonies were planted at the expense of Parliament and that therefore the Parliament has a right to tax them. The truth is that they were planted at the expense of private adventurers who went over there to settle, with leave of the King, given by charter.

COMMITMENT

⇢ Relation without friendship, friendship without power, power without will, will without virtue are not worth a fart.

COMMITTEES

⇢ We are sent to consult—not to contend with each other, and make a declaration of fixed opinion, and of determined resolution never to change it which neither enlighten or convince us. Harmony and union are necessary to give weight to our councils and render them effectual in promotion and securing the common goods.

COMMON MAN

⇢ There have been as many great souls unknown to fame as any of the most famous.

COMMON SENSE

⇢ Tim was so learned he could name a horse in nine languages. So ignorant that he bought a cow to ride on.

⇢ A learned blockhead is a greater blockhead than an ignorant one.

⇢ Good sense is a thing all need, few have, and none think they lack.

COMPANIONS

⇢ He that lieth down with dogs, shall rise up with fleas.

COMPANIONSHIP

⇢ The rotten apple spoils his companions.

COMPLAINT

↬ The tongue ever turns to the aching tooth.

↬ Let thy discontents be secret.

CONSCIENCE

↬ A quiet conscience sleeps in thunder.

CONSERVATISM

↬ Whenever we attempt to mend the scheme of Providence and to interfere in the Government of the world, we had need be very circumspect lest we do more harm than good.

CONSTITUTION

↬ If any form of government is capable of making a nation happy, ours I think bids fair now for producing that effect. But after all much depends upon the people who are governed.

↬ Our constitution is now established and has an appearance that promises permanency.

↬ Sir, I agree to this Constitution with all its faults, if they are such, because I think a general government [is] necessary for us and there is no form of government but what may be a blessing to the people if well administered. Thus, I consent, Sir, to this Constitution not because I expect no better [but rather] because I am not sure it is not the best.[7]

---

[7] This is the essence of Franklin's concluding remarks to the Constitutional Convention in 1787.

∽ So great is the unanimity, we hear, that prevails in the Convention upon all great federal subjects, that it has been proposed to call the rooms in which they assemble—Unanimity Hall.

CONTINENTAL CONGRESS
∽ I look on the dignity of the American Congress equal to any assembly on earth.

CONVERSATION
∽ Speak not but what may benefit others or yourself; avoid trifling conversation.

COSMETICS
∽ As to rouge, they [French Ladies] don't pretend to imitate nature in laying it on—cut a hole of paper three inches in diameter and put it on side of your face—then with brush dip in color, paint face, and paper together, when the paper is taken off—a round patch of red.

COURTESY
∽ To be humble to superiors is duty; to equals, is courtesy; to inferiors, nobleness.

COURTIER
∽ He that would rise at court must begin by creeping.

CRAFTSMAN
∽ He that has a trade has an office of profit and honor.

∽ Learn from the skillful: He that teaches himself hath a fool for his master.

CREATIVITY

∽ The Muses love the morning.

∽ *Give me the Muse whose generous force*
Impatient of the reins
Pursues an unattempted course
Breaks all the critics' iron chains.

∽ A full belly makes a dull brain.

CREDITORS

∽ Money that is owed is an estate in the clouds.

∽ Creditors are a superstitious set, great observers of set days and times.

CRITICISM

∽ Love your enemies; for they shall tell you all your faults.

∽ The sting of a reproach is the truth of it.

∽ One cannot behave so as to obtain the esteem of the wise and good, without drawing on one's self at the same time the envy and malice of the foolish and wicked, and the latter is a testimony of the former.

CULTURES

∽ Perhaps if we could examine the manner of different nations with impartiality, we should find no people so rude as to be without rules of politeness, nor any so polite as not to have some remains of rudeness.

CUNNING

❧ A cunning man is overmatched by a cunning and a half.

DANGER

❧ 'Tis very ill driving black hogs in the dark.

DAUGHTER

❧ *My son is a son till he takes him a wife,*
But my daughter's a daughter all the days of my life.

DEATH

❧ I look upon death to be as necessary to our constitution as sleep. We shall rise refreshed in the morning.

❧ Methinks life should have a dramatic ending like a stage piece.

❧ A dying man can do nothing easy.

❧ And it is right that we should meet with something [physical suffering] to wean us from this world, and make us willing, when called to leave it. Otherwise the parting would indeed be grievous.

DEBT

❧ Pay what you owe and you'll know what is your own.

DEBTORS

❧ Creditors have better memories than debtors.

DECEIT

… You may be too cunning for one but not for all.[8]

DEFENSE

… One sword keeps another in the scabbard.

… It is absurd pretending to be the lovers of liberty while they grudge paying for the defense of it.

DEISM

… As man is part of this great machine, the Universe, his regular acting is requisite to the regular moving of the whole.

DEMOCRACY

… If . . . we have not wisdom enough to govern ourselves, we will strengthen the opinion . . . that popular governments cannot long support themselves.[9]

DESPAIR

… Industry pays debts, while despair increases them.

DICTATOR

… There are three great destroyers of mankind: plague, famine and a Hero [demagogue]. Plagues and famines destroy persons only and leave your goods to your heirs, but a Hero, when he comes,

---

[8] Abraham Lincoln improved on that when he said, "You can fool all the people some of the time, and some of the people all the time, but you can't fool all the people all the time."

[9] Abraham Lincoln would strike this theme in his Gettysburg Address.

takes life and goods together; his business and glory of it is to destroy men and works of man.

DICTIONARY

☞ In your common reading, I think it would be well for you to have a good dictionary at hand.

DIETING

☞ To lengthen thy life, lessen thy meals.

☞ Three good (big) meals a day is bad living.

☞ Eat to live—not live to eat.

☞ Fat kitchen—lean will.

☞ Many dishes, many diseases.

☞ *Cheese and salt meat*
Should be sparingly cut.

DILIGENCE

☞ He that rises late must trot all day.

☞ Diligence is the mother of good luck.

☞ At the working man's house, hunger looks in but dares not enter.

☞ *Plow deep while sluggards sleep*
And you'll have corn to sell and keep.

DIPLOMACY

↪ Tart words make no friends; a spoonful of honey will catch more flies than vinegar.

DISASTER INSURANCE

↪ I have sometimes thought that it might be well to establish an office of insurance for farmers against the damage that may occur to them from storms, blights, insects, etc.

DISCIPLINE

↪ Deny self for self's sake.

DISCRETION

↪ Be civil to all; sociable to many; familiar with few; friend to one; enemy to none.

↪ Never contradict another.[10]

DO-IT-YOURSELF

↪ If you would have it done, go; if not, send.

DOGMATISM

↪ Singularity in the right has ruined many.

↪ My doxy is your heterodoxy.

---

[10] Thomas Jefferson said that this advice was the secret of Franklin's persuasive powers. He reported he never heard Franklin directly contradict anyone.

DONOR

☞ He gives twice who gives quickly—for he will soon be called on to give again.

DRESS

☞ Eat to please yourself; dress to please others.

DRIVE

☞ All our different desires and passions proceed from and are reducible to this one point *uneasiness* though the means we propose to ourselves for expelling it are infinite. One [is] *Fame,* another *Wealth,* a third *Power* as the means to gain this end.

DUTCH

☞ The Dutch would fain save all the money that they touch.

EDITING

☞ I have made it a rule to avoid becoming a draftsman of papers to be reviewed by a public body [committee].[11]

☞ He has drawn the teeth and pared the nails of my paper so that it can neither scratch nor bite.

EDUCATION

☞ I think with you that nothing is more important for the public weal than to train up youth in wisdom and virtue. Wise and

---

[11] Franklin was explaining why he rejected the chance to write the Declaration of Independence. He proposed Jefferson as the drafter.

good men are, in my opinion, the strength of a state far more than riches or arms.

☞ Learning whether speculative or practical is . . . the natural source of wealth and honor.

☞ He that lives well is learned enough.

☞ Knowledge and Learning is to be cultivated and Ignorance dissipated.

☞ As to their studies, it would be well if they could be taught everything that is *useful* and everything that is *ornamental*. But art is long and time is short. It is therefore proposed that they be taught things that are *most* useful and *most* ornamental—in regard to the professions for which they are intended.

Educate and inform the whole mass of the people. Enable them to see that it is their interest to preserve peace and order and they will preserve them. They are the only sure reliance for the preservation of our liberty.

☞ The good education of youth has been esteemed by wise men in all ages, on the surest foundation of the happiness both in private families and of Commonwealths [states].

EFFORT
☞ There are no gains without pains.

EGOTISM
☞ He that falls in love with himself will have no rivals.

EIGHTEENTH CENTURY

‣ This is the age of experiment.

EMPIRE

‣ An Empire, like a cake, is most easily diminished at the edges.

EMPLOYMENT

‣ When men are employed, they are best contented; for on the days they worked, they were good-natured and cheerful and with the consciousness of having done a good day's work, they spent the evening jollily; but on idle days they were mutinous and quarrelsome.[12]

ENEMY

‣ *The weakest foe boasts some revenging Power*
The weakest friend some serviceable hour.

‣ There is no little enemy.

‣ I wish every kind of prosperity to my friends and I forgive my enemies.

ENGLISH LANGUAGE

‣ We have more words than nations—we have a dozen words for the same thing.

---

[12] Franklin made this observation while he supervised the erection of a fort by the Moravians near Bethlehem.

ETHICS

❧ O that moral science were in a fair way of improvement that men would cease to be wolves to one another and that human beings would at length learn what they now improperly call humanity.

EXAMPLE

❧ Keep your mouth wet and your feet dry.

❧ Setting too good an example is a kind of slander seldom forgiven.

❧ A good example is the best sermon.

❧ None preaches better than the ant and she says nothing.

EXERCISE

❧ Exercise [is] to be measured not by the time or by distance but by those degrees of warmth it produces in the body. There is more exercise in one mile's walking on foot than in five on horseback . . . there is more exercise in walking one mile up and down stairs than in five on a level floor.

❧ By the use of the dumbbell, I have in forty swings quickened my pulse from sixty to a hundred beats a minute counted by a stopwatch.

❧ The poor man must walk to get meat for his stomach—the rich man to get stomach to his meat.

❧ I walk a league every day in my chamber. I walk quick and for an hour or so—so that I go a league. I make a point of religion about it.

EXPENSES

☞ When people's incomes are lessened, if they cannot proportionately lessen their outgoings, they must come to poverty.[13]

EXPERIENCE

☞ Experience keeps a dear school, but fools will learn in no other.

☞ The things which hurt instruct.

FACTS

☞ If you will not hear Reason, She'll surely rap your knuckles.

FAITH

☞ The way to see by Faith is to shut the eye of Reason.

FAMILY

☞ Above all I dislike family quarrels and when they happen among my relations nothing gives me more pain.

FARMER

☞ A plowman on his legs is higher than a gentleman on his knees.

---

[13] From a letter to his wife Deborah.

❧ I think agriculture the most noble of all employments, being the most independent.

❧ *Happy the man whose wish and care*
A few paternal acres bound
Content to breathe his native air
In his own ground.

FASHION
❧ *Fond pride of dress is sure a very curse*
Ee'r fancy you consult, consult your purse.

FASTING
❧ Eat few suppers and you'll need few medicines.

❧ Dine with little, sup with less, do better still, sleep supperless.

FELLOWSHIP
❧ For my own part I find I love company, chat, a laugh, a glass, even a song as well as ever.

FIGHT
❧ I remember when I was a boxing boy, it was allowed, even after an adversary said he had enough, to give him a final blow. Let ours be a doozy.[14]

---

[14] Franklin is writing at the end of the War for Independence.

28

FLATTERY

- ❧ Approve not of him who commends all you have to say.

- ❧ The honey is sweet, but the bee has a sting.

- ❧ *A flatterer never seems absurd*
  The flattered always takes his word.

FOREIGN POLICY

- ❧ Our credit and weight in Europe depend more on what we do than what we say.

FORTUNE

- ❧ He that waits upon fortune is never sure of a dinner.

FREEDOM

- ❧ If we tamely give up our rights in this contest, a century to come will not restore us in the opinion of the world; we shall be stamped with the character of poltroons and fools and be despised and trampled upon, not by this haughty, insolent nation but by all mankind.

FREEDOM OF THE PRESS

- ❧ Liberty of the Cudgel.

- ❧ It is a principle among printers that when truth has fair play, it will always prevail over falsehood; therefore, though they have undoubted property in their own press, yet they willingly allow that anyone is entitled to the use of it.

꘏ Grievances cannot be redressed unless they are known and they cannot be known but through complaints and petitions. If they are deemed affronts and the messengers punished as offenders, who will henceforth send petitions?

꘏ If the liberty of the press were understood as merely the liberty of discussing the propriety of public measures and political opinions, let us have as much of it as you please. But if it means the liberty of affronting, columnizing, and defaming one another, I, for my part, own myself willing to part with my share of it.

FREEDOM OF SPEECH
꘏ Without freedom of thought there can be no such thing as wisdom and no such thing as public liberty without freedom of speech.

꘏ Whoever would overthrow the liberty of a nation must begin by subduing freeness of speech.

FREE TRADE
꘏ I would observe that commerce—the more free and unrestrained it is—the better.

FRENCH
꘏ They have some frivolities, but they are harmless. To dress their heads so that a hat cannot be put on them, and then wear their hats under the arms, and to fill their noses with tobacco may be called follies but they are not vices.

FRENCH WOMEN

☞ Somebody, it seems, gave it out that I loved ladies; and then everybody presented me their ladies (or the ladies presented themselves) to be *embraced,* that is to have their necks kissed. For as to kissing of lips and cheeks, it is not the mode here, the first is reckoned rude and the other may rub off the paint. The French ladies have, however, a thousand other ways of rendering themselves agreeable.

FRESH AIR

☞ Another means of preserving health . . . is having a constant supply of fresh air in your bedchamber. It has been a great mistake [to do] the sleeping in rooms exactly closed, and in beds surrounded by curtains. No outward air that may come in to you is so unwholesome as the unchanged air, so often breathed of a close chamber.

FRIENDSHIP

☞ To be intimate with a foolish friend is like going to bed with a razor.

☞ If you would be loved, love and be lovable.

☞ Let us keep the chain from rusting.

☞ Be slow to choose a friend—slower in changing.

☞ *He that drinks his cider alone*
  Let him catch his horse alone.

FRONTIER

↬ So vast is the territory of North America that it will require many ages to settle it fully—and till it is fully settled, labor will never be cheap here, where no man continues long a laborer for others.

FRUGALITY

↬ He that burns logs that cost nothing is twice warmed.

GENEROSITY

↬ A man is sometimes more generous when he has but a little money than he who has plenty, perhaps through fear of being thought to have but little.

GENIUS

↬ A fine genius, in his own country, is like gold in a mine.

GENTLEMAN

↬ Money and good manners make the gentleman.

GLIBNESS

↬ Here comes a glib tongue who can outflatter a dedication and lie like ten epitaphs.

GOD

↬ The longer I live, the more convincing proofs I see of this truth: that God governs in the affairs of men.

↬ Fear of the Lord is the beginning of wisdom.

GOOD TIMES

◦ In bad fortune I hope for the good; in good I fear the bad.

GOSSIP

◦ I resolved to speak ill of no man whatever, not even in the matter of truth but rather, by some means, excuse the faults I hear charged upon others and upon proper occasions speak all the good I know of everybody.

◦ Use no hurtful deceit, think candidly and justly, and if you speak, speak accordingly.

GOUT

◦ You [gout] would not only torment my body to death, but ruin my good name; you [gout] reproach me as a glutton and tippler and all the world knows I am neither one nor the other.

GOVERNMENT

◦ In rivers and bad government the lightest things swim to the top.

◦ The first mistake of public business is going into it.

GOVERNMENT SPENDING

◦ The King's cheese is half wasted in parings—but no matter, 'tis made of people's milk!

GRACE

◦ Hast thou virtue? Acquire also the graces and beauties of virtue.

GRIEF

☞ Natural affections must have their course. The best remedy of grief is time.

GULLIBILITY

☞ In this world men are saved not by faith but by the lack of it.

HABITS

☞ 'Tis easier to prevent bad habits than to break them.

☞ Many people lead bad lives that would gladly lead good ones but do not know how to make the change.

HAPPINESS

☞ It is enough for good minds to be affected by other people's misfortunes—but they that are vexed at everybody's good luck can never be happy.

☞ Human felicity is produced not so much by great pieces of good fortune that seldom happen, as by little advantages that occur every day.

☞ Happiness depends more on judgment of one's own self.

HARD WORK

☞ The cat in gloves catches no mice.

HEALTH

☞ Nine men in ten are suicides.

HEATING

☙ Warm rooms make people apt to catch a cold.

HISTORIANS

☙ Historians relate, not so much what is done, as to what they would have believed.

☙ This much I thought necessary to say in favor of an honest set of writers, collecting and supporting and supplying the printers with news . . . the infinite advantage of all future Livys, Rapins, Robertsons, Humes, Smollets, and Macaulays who may be sincerely inclined to furnish the world with that *rara avis,* a true history.

HISTORY

☙ Be mindful of the past.

☙ Let them now begin to read history.

HONOR

☙ That I may have a constant regard to honor and probity, that I may possess a perfect innocence and a good conscience and at length become truly virtuous and magnanimous—help me, Good God, help me, O Father.

HUMANITY

☙ What good shall I do this day? I would rather have it said "He lived usefully" than "He died rich."

☙ Wrong none by doing injuries, or omitting the benefits that are your duty.

☞ Is there a pleasure upon Earth to be compared with that which arises from the sense of making others happy?

HUMILITY

☞ After crosses and losses men grow humbler and wiser.

☞ Imitate Jesus and Socrates.

HUMOR

☞ Your story is well told and entertaining. Only let me admonish you of a small though common fault of storytellers. You should not have introduced it by telling me *how comical* 'twas. For when the expectation is raised too high, 'tis a disadvantage to the thing expected.

HUSBAND

☞ One good husband is worth two good wives; for the scarcer things are, the more they're valued.

IDEALISM

☞ Though I never arrived at the perfection I had been so ambitious of obtaining, yet I was, by the endeavor, a better and happier man than I otherwise should have been if I had not attempted it.

IDLENESS

☞ Idleness is the Dead Sea that swallows all virtues.

☞ Sloth, like rust, consumes faster than labor wears.

꘎ Trouble springs from idleness, and grievous toil from needless ease.

꘎ Be always ashamed to catch thyself idle.

꘎ God gives all things to industry.

IMMIGRANTS

꘎ Wherever Liberty shines, there people will naturally flock to bask themselves in its beams.

꘎ I'm going from the old world to the new; and I fancy I feel like those who are leaving this world for the new; grief at the parting; fear of the passage; hope for the future.

INDEPENDENCE

꘎ Content to live, content to die unknown, Lord of myself, accountable to none.

INDIANS

꘎ The dying shrieks and groans of the murdered will often sound in your ears.[15]

꘎ If an Indian injures me does it follow that I may revenge that injury on all Indians?

---

[15] Franklin was attacking a central Pennsylvania Scotch-Irish massacre of innocent Indians.

INDISCRETION

❧ The tongue offends and the ears get the cuffing.

INDUSTRY

❧ Industry needs not wish.

INFLUENZA

❧ Cold water, drunk plentifully, is good for a fever.

INHERITANCE

❧ Remember whatever a child saves of his parents' money will be his in another day.

INJUSTICE

❧ Laws, like cobwebs, catch small flies. Great ones break through before your eyes.

INNOCENCE

❧ Innocence is its own defense.

INSURANCE

❧ The many make good the losses of the few.

INSURANCE MUTUALS

❧ I am humbly of the opinion that the country is ripe for many such friendly [insurance] societies, whereby every man might help another, without any disservice to himself.

INTEGRITY

❧ I grew convinced that truth, sincerity, and integrity in dealing between man and man were of utmost importance to the felicity of life.

INTELLECTUALS

∽ The most exquisite folly is that of wisdom spun too fine.

∽ You philosophers are sages in your maxims and fools in your conduct.

∽ To be proud of knowledge is to be blind with light.

∽ Most of learning in use, is of no great use.

INVENTION

∽ We should be glad of an opportunity to serve others by any invention of ours and this we should do freely and generously.[16]

INVESTMENT

∽ Money can beget money.

IRELAND

∽ The misery and distress which your ill-fated country has been so frequently exposed to, and has so often experienced by such a combination of rapine treachery and violence as would have disgraced the name of government, have most sincerely affected your friends in America and have engaged the most serious attention of Congress.

[16] Franklin was explaining why he never applied for patents on his inventions.

∽ I have found them to be disposed to be friends of America—there are many brave spirits among them.

JUDGMENT
∽ Many complain of their memory, few of their judgment.

JUDGMENTAL
∽ To be sensible of our own faults is good, for it leads us to avoid them in future; but to be sensitive to and afflicted by the faults of other people is not good.

JUSTICE
∽ Laws too gentle are seldom obeyed; too severe, seldom executed.

KINGS
∽ Kings and bears often worry their keepers.

LANGUAGE
∽ Write with the learned; pronounce with the vulgar.

LAW
∽ In some countries the course of the courts is so tedious that the remedy of justice is worse than injustice.

LAWSUIT
∽ A lean award is better than a fat judgment.

LAWYERS
∽ Lawyers can with ease twist words and meanings as they please.

∽ Necessity knows no law; I know some attorneys of the same.

∽ A country man between two lawyers is like a fish between two cats.

∽ A good lawyer, a bad neighbor.

∽ Don't misinform your doctor nor your lawyer.

∽ *God works wonders now and then;*
  Behold a lawyer, an honest man!

LAZINESS
∽ Laziness travels so slowly that poverty soon overtakes him.

LEADERSHIP
∽ He that cannot obey, cannot command.

∽ Leaders who little know, little grow.

LEGISLATOR
∽ I should be ready to swear never to serve again as an Assemblyman since both sides expect more from me than they ought.[17]

LEISURE
∽ Employ thy time well, if thou meanest to gain leisure.

---

[17] Franklin was commenting on his years as a Pennsylvania legislator.

∽ Leisure is the time for doing something useful.

LIBERTY

∽ Liberty best thrives in the woods.

∽ Where liberty is, there is my country.

∽ They that give up essential liberty to obtain a little temporary safety deserve neither liberty or safety.

∽ God grant that not only the love of liberty, but a thorough knowledge of the rights of man, may pervade all the nations of the earth so that a philosopher may set his foot anywhere on its surface and say, "this is my country."[18]

LIBRARY

∽ *{He} who values nothing that's within*
  Buys books as men hunt beavers—for their skin.

LIE

∽ Half the truth is often a great lie.

LIFE

∽ I have no objection to a repetition of my life from its beginning, only asking the advantages authors have in a second edition—to correct its faults.

---

[18] A quotation often attributed to Franklin is "Where freedom is, there is my country"—actually this is the basis for that apocryphal quotation.

❧ Live as if you are to live forever.

❧ *If you would not be forgotten*
  As soon as you are dead and rotten
  Either write things worth reading
  Or do things worth the writing.

❧ *Learn, wretches, learn the motions of the mind*
  Why you were made, for what you were designed
  And the great moral end of humankind.

LISTENER
❧ A pair of ears will drain a hundred tongues.

❧ Speech and speed—the closed mouth catches no flies.

LOOKS
❧ I believe that long habits of virtue have a sensible effect on the countenance.

LOQUACITY
❧ He that speaks much, is much mistaken.

LOVE
❧ Love, cough, and smoke can't be well hid.

❧ If Jack's in love, he's no judge of Jill's beauty.

LUCK
❧ Diligence is the mother of good luck.

LUST

ʗɢ Samson with his strong body had a weak head, or he would have not laid in a harlot's lap.

ʗɢ He that lives carnally will not live eternally.

ʗɢ Beauty and folly are old companions.

ʗɢ Rarely use venery but for health and offspring; never to dullness, weakness, or the injury of your own or another's face or reputation.

LUXURIES

ʗɢ Buy what thou hast no need of, and ere long thou shalt sell thy necessities.

MADEIRA (*A Sweet Dessert Wine*)

ʗɢ You will say my advice smelled of Madeira. You are right.[19]

ʗɢ I should prefer to any ordinary death the being immersed in a cask of Madeira with a few friends till that time, to be then recalled to life by the solar warmth of my death country!

MAGNA CARTA

ʗɢ This kingdom [England] is a good deal indebted for its liberties to the public spirit of the ancient clergy who joined with the barons.

---

[19] Franklin was generally abstemious but he did enjoy Madeira, a fortified white wine.

MALCONTENTS

∞ Discontented minds and fevers of the body are not cured by changing beds or business.

MANAGEMENT

∞ Not to oversee workmen is to leave your purse open.

∞ Beware of little expenses, a small leak will sink a great ship.

∞ Keep care of the shop and the shop will keep care of you.

∞ Let all things have their places; let each part of your business have its time.

MANKIND

∞ Mankind are very odd creatures; one half censure what they practice; the other half practice what they censure; the rest always say and do as they ought.

MANNERS

∞ He is not well-bred that cannot bear ill-breeding in others.

MARRIAGE

∞ The married state, after all our jokes, is the happiest. Man and woman have each of them qualities and tempers, in which the other is deficient. Single and separate, they are not a complete human being; they are like odd halves of scissors.

∞ Keep your eyes open before marriage—afterwards keep them half shut.

∞ Many unhappy marriages are occasioned by mercenary views in one or both of the parties.

∞ He who takes a wife, takes care.

∞ Where there is a marriage without love—there will be a love without marriage.

∞ Never take a wife until you have a house to put her in.

∞ A house without a woman and firelight is like a body without soul and spirit.

MATERIALISM

∞ Wealth and content are not always bedfellows.

∞ If riches are yours, why not take them to the other world?

∞ He does not possess wealth; it possesses him.

∞ Happiness in this world depends on internals, not externals.

∞ Avarice and happiness never saw each other; how then should they be acquainted?

∞ *Content and Riches seldom meet together*
   Riches take thou, contentment I'd rather.

MATURITY

∞ An old young man will be a young old man.

MEN

☞ Old boys have their playthings as well as young ones—the difference is only their price.

MERETRICIOUS

☞ She lends out her tail and borrows her face.

MISFORTUNE

☞ A change of fortune hurts a Wise Man no more than the change of the moon.

☞ To bear other people's afflictions every one has courage enough to spare.

MISTAKES

☞ *A slip of the foot you may soon recover*
—but a slip of the tongue you may never get over.

MOB

☞ A mob's a monster; heads enough but no brains.

MODERATION

☞ Kill no more pigeons than you can eat.

MODESTY

☞ A lack of modesty is a lack of good sense.

MONEY

☞ Wealth is not his that has it, but his that enjoys it.

☞ The use of money is all the advantage there is in having money.

☞ After getting the first hundred pounds, it is more easy to get the second.

☞ He that is of the opinion money will do everything may well be suspected of doing everything for money.

MOTHER
☞ Where yet was ever found the mother who'd exchange her boob son!

MOVING
☞ Three removes [moving] are as bad as a fire.

NATION
☞ A nation, to keep respect of other states, must keep its own self-respect at home.

☞ Happy is the nation—whose history is not diverting [amusing].

NEATNESS
☞ Sloth, like rust, consumes faster than labor wears.

NEGOTIATION
☞ Necessity never made a good bargain.

☞ When one has so many different people with different opinions to deal with . . . one is obliged to give in on smaller points in order to gain the greater.

◌➤ If you have no honey in your pot, have some in your mouth.

◌➤ He who speaks ill of the mare, will buy her.

NEW JERSEY
◌➤ A barrel with bungs [lids] at both ends.[20]

NEW YEAR'S RESOLUTIONS
◌➤ *With the old Almanac and the old year,*
  Leave the old vices, tho' ever so dear.

NOSTALGIA
◌➤ The golden age was never the present age.

NUDISM
◌➤ I rise almost every morning and sit in my chamber without any clothes whatever, half an hour or an hour, according to the season—either reading or writing.

OFFICE
◌➤ I shall never ask, never refuse, nor ever resign an office.[21]

---

[20] Franklin was describing the problem of New Jersey, which was dominated by New York City to the north and Philadelphia to the south.

[21] Franklin said this when offered by the Continental Congress the postmaster generalship of the colonies in 1775—a post which he had earlier held as the colonial postmaster general.

OLD AGE

❧ As having their own way is one of the greatest comforts of life to old people, I think their friends should accommodate them in that.

❧ I have, thanks to God, a competency, for the little time I may expect to live, and am grown too old for ambition of every other kind but that of leaving a good name behind me.

❧ An old man in the house is a good sign.

❧ Losing our friends, those one by one, is the tax we pay for long living, and it is a heavy one.

❧ I seem to have intrigued myself into the company of posterity.

❧ At that age [youth] the spirit is exterior, at mine it is interior.

❧ People who live a long life and drink to the bottom of the cup must expect to meet some of the dregs.

❧ One way of being content with the situation is comparing it with a worse.

❧ The fewer we [the old] become, the more let us love one another.

❧ Nothing is more apt to sour the temper of aged people than indifference and lack of respect.

❧ By my rambling digressions, I perceive myself to be getting old.

ᵒ All would live long but none would be old.

ᵒ Anxiety begins to disturb my rest, and whatever robs an old man of his sleep, soon demolishes him.

ONIONS
ᵒ Onions can make even heirs and widows weep.

OPINION
ᵒ The opinions of men are almost as various as their faces.

OPPORTUNITY
ᵒ I think she [Britain] has neither the temper nor the wisdom to seize the golden opportunity.[22]

OPPOSITION
ᵒ I take it that clamor is at present our best policy.

ᵒ Popular opposition to a public measure is no proof of its impropriety even though the opposition be excited and headed by men of distinction.

ORATOR
ᵒ History will show the wonderful effects of oratory in governing, and leading bodies of mankind, armies, cities, nations.

---

[22] Franklin is describing Britain in July 1775.

✎ Political oratory is being chiefly performed [today] by the pen and press—its advantage . . . is that its effects are more lasting.

ORPHANS

✎ Late children, early orphans.

OSTENTATION

✎ *In prosperous fortunes be modest and wise*
  The greatest may fall, and the lowest may rise.

OVERCONFIDENCE

✎ Let us beware of every word and action that may betray a confidence in its success, lest we render ourselves ridiculous in case of disappointment.

PARENT

✎ There is no rank in natural knowledge of equal dignity and importance with that of being a good parent.

PARTY LOYALTY

✎ There are natural duties which precede political ones and cannot be extinguished by them.

PATENT MEDICINE

✎ Quacks are the greatest liars in the world except for the patients who extol their medicines.

PATENTS

✎ We should be glad of an opportunity to serve others by an invention of ours, and this we should do freely and generously.

PATIENCE

∿ He that can have patience can have what he will.

PEACE

∿ There never was a good war or bad peace.

∿ At length we are in peace, God be praised. And long, very long may it continue. All wars are follies, very expensive and very mischievous ones. When will mankind be convinced of this and agree to settle their difference by arbitration?

∿ Blessed are the peacemakers—for in this they are frequently cursed.

∿ The way to secure peace is to be prepared for war.

PERSISTENCE

∿ Little strokes fell great oaks.

∿ Constant dropping wears away stones.

PERSUASION

∿ If you want to convince, speak of interest, not of reason.

PHILOSOPHY

∿ What signifies philosophy that does not apply to some use?

PHYSICIANS

∿ God heals and the doctor takes the fee.

∿ He is a good man who makes his doctor his heir.

∞ Beware of the young doctor and old barber.

∞ He is the best physician who knows the worthlessness of most medicines.

∞ Disease was intended as the punishment of intemperance, sloth, and other vices and the example of that punishment was intended to promote and strengthen the opposite virtues. But here you step in, officiously with your art and disappoint those wise intentions of nature, and make man safe in their excesses.

PLANNING
∞ Forewarned is forearmed.

∞ Don't think to hunt two hares with one dog.

PLAYBOY
∞ *Women and wine, game and deceit*
Make the wealth small and the want great.

PLEASURE
∞ The honest man takes pains and then enjoys pleasure; the knave takes pleasure and then suffers pain.

∞ Pleasure is that satisfaction which arises in the mind upon and is caused by the accomplishments of desire.

POLITICIANS
∞ Here comes the orator with his flood of words and drop of reason.

◌ Here comes the glib tongue—who can outflatter a dedication and lie like ten epitaphs.

◌ Few in public affairs act from a mere view of the good of their country whatever they may pretend . . . fewer still act with a view to the good of mankind.

◌ Speak the exact truth to politicians. That is my only cunning. Politicians are so corrupt that I can always fool them that way.

◌ There are two passions which have a powerful influence in the affairs of men—a love of power and a love of money.

POLITICS
◌ *Free from the rage of party zeal*
  All those we love who seek the public weal.

POMPOSITY
◌ Even he who sits on the highest throne sits on his own ass.

POPULAR OPINION
◌ I can only judge what other people will think and how they will act, by what I feel within myself.

◌ Passion governs, and she never governs wisely.

◌ The feeble voice of those groveling passions cannot extend so far in time.

POVERTY
◌ Having been poor is no shame, but being ashamed of it is.

⚹ It is hard for an empty sack to stand upright.

POWER

⚹ Sudden power is apt to be insolent, sudden liberty saucy—
that behaves best which has grown gradually.

⚹ Many princes sin with David; but few repent with him.

PRAYER

⚹ Work as if you will live a hundred years. Pray as if you would
die tomorrow.

PREACHERS

⚹ An advantage that itinerant preachers have over those who are
stationary preachers—the latter cannot easily improve their deliv-
ery of a sermon by so many rehearsals.

PREGNANCY

⚹ A ship under sail and a big-bellied woman are the handsomest
two things that can be seen in common.

PREJUDICE

⚹ He who removes a prejudice or an error from our minds, con-
tributes to their beauty as he would do to that of our faces who
should clear them of a wart on men.

PREPAREDNESS

⚹ Let us beware of being lulled into a dangerous security of
being weakened by internal contentions and divisions; of neglect in

military exercises and disciplines in providing stores of arms and munitions of war; for the expenses required to prevent a war are much lighter than those that will, if not prevented, be necessary to maintain it.

PRESS
∞ Those who follow printing are scarce able to do anything which shall not probably give offense to some and perhaps to many.

PRETENTIOUSNESS
∞ If your head is wax, don't walk in the sun.

PREVENTION
∞ The way to be safe is never to be secure.

PREVENTIVE MEDICINE
∞ Be not sick too late, nor well too soon.

PRIDE
∞ The proud hate pride—in others.

∞ Pride is as loud a beggar as Need, and a great deal more saucy.

∞ There is perhaps no one of our natural passions so hard to subdue as pride. Disguise it, struggle with it, stifle it, and mortify it.

∞ Pride dines on vanity and sups on contempt.

PRIG
∞ A man without faults is a hateful creature.

∞ I think I like a speckled character best.

PRIGGISHNESS
∞ To be proud of virtue is to poison yourself with the antidote.

PRINTERS
∞ Printers are educated in the belief that when men differ in opinion, both sides ought equally to have the advantage of being heard by the public; and that when truth and error have fair play, the former is always an overmatch for the latter; hence they cheerfully serve all contending writers that pay them well, without regard which side they are of the question in dispute.

PRISON
∞ There never was an ugly love or handsome prison.

PROBLEMS
∞ Great affairs sometimes take their rise from small circumstances.

∞ Weighty questions ask for deliberate answers.

PROCRASTINATION
∞ Never leave that till tomorrow which you can do today.

∞ One today is worth two tomorrows.

PROMISCUITY
∞ Light-heeled mothers make leaden-heeled daughters.

∽ She that paints her face thinks of her tail.

PROMISES
∽ Endeavor to speak truth in every instance—to give nobody expectations that are not likely to be answered.

PROPERTY
∽ Mine is better than ours.

PROSECUTOR
∽ The shepherd drives the wolf from the sheep's throat, for which the sheep thanks the shepherd as a liberator, while the wolf denounces him as a destroyer of liberty.

PROTEST
∽ The waves do not rise but when the winds blow.

PUBLIC OPINION
∽ The strength of government depends on the opinion of the people.

PUBLIC POLICY
∽ The best public measures are seldom adopted from previous wisdom but forced by the occasion.

∽ If you can promote the prosperity of your people, and leave them happier than you found them, whatever your principles are, your memory will be honored.

PUBLIC RELATIONS

⁍ Now by press we can speak to nations. And good books and well-written pamphlets have great and general influence. The facility with which the same truths may be repeatedly enforced by placing them daily in different lights in newspapers—which are everywhere read—gives a great chance of establishing them. And we now find that it is not only right to strike while the iron is hot, but that it may be very practical to heat it by continuous striking.

⁍ Never spare the parson's wine or the baker's pudding.

PUBLIC SERVICE

⁍ Your slightest indiscretions will be magnified into crimes.

⁍ The public is often niggardly, even of its thanks, while you are sure of being censured by malevolent critics.

PURPOSE

⁍ Think of three things: whence you came, where you are going, and to whom you must account.

QUARREL

⁍ In differences among friends, they that make the first concessions are the wisest.

⁍ *Quarrels never could last long*
If one side only the wrong.

REACTIONARY

☞ There is in mankind an unaccountable prejudice in favor of ancient customs and habitudes which inclines to a continuance of them after circumstances which formerly made them useful cease to exist.

READING (YOUTH)

☞ Let lessons for reading be varied that the youth may be acquainted with good style of all kinds of prose and verse—a well-told story, a piece of sermon, a general's speech to his troops, a speech in a tragedy, some part of a comedy, an ode, a satire or blank verse.

REASON

☞ The chief faculty in a man is his reason and consequently his chief good . . . consists not merely in action but reasonable action.

REASONS

☞ It is common for men to give pretended reasons instead of one real one.

REBELLION

☞ You can see that I am warm [passionate]. If a temper naturally cool and phlegmatic, in old age, can be thus heated, you will judge by that of the general temper here, which is a little short of madness.[23]

---

[23] Franklin is describing the passions of the Continental Congress in May 1776.

‰ Between nations every injury is not worth a war, so between the governed and the governing every mistake in government, every encroachment on rights is not worth a rebellion.

REFORM

‰ Men take more trouble to mask than mend.

‰ To get the bad customs of a country changed, and new ones, though better, introduced, it is necessary first to remove the prejudices of the people, enlighten their ignorance, and convince them that their interests will be promoted by the proposed changes; and this is not the work of a day.

‰ *By these I swear (be witness Earth and Skies)*
  Fair order shall from confusion rise.

RELATIVES

‰ Visit your Aunt but not every night; call on your brothers but not every day.

RELIGION

‰ Wise men wonder at the present growth of infidelity [godlessness].

‰ Many have quarreled about Religion, that never practiced it.

‰ If men are so wicked with religion, what would they be without it?

‰ Lighthouses are more helpful than churches.

 ☞ I think vital religion has always suffered when orthodoxy is more regarded than virtue.

RENEWAL
 ☞ We'll do as married people do—tire and begin again.

REPUTATION
 ☞ Glass, china, and reputation are easily cracked and never well mended.

RESOLUTION
 ☞ Resolve to perform what you ought; perform without fail what you resolve.

RETIREMENT
 ☞ There are times in which the post of honor is a private station.

REVENGE
 ☞ There's small revenge in words but words may be greatly revenged.

REVOLUTION
 ☞ Does not so atrocious a conduct [by King George III] toward his subjects dissolve their allegiance?

RISK
 ☞ *Vessels large may venture more,*
   But little boats keep near shore.

SALARIES (OF POLITICIANS)

✑ We should not make places of honor places of profit.

SAVINGS

✑ A penny saved is a penny earned.

✑ A man may—if he knows not how to save as he gets—keep his nose to the grindstone.

✑ When the well is dry, they know the worth of water.

✑ For age and want, save while you may; no morning sun lasts a whole day.

SCIENCE

✑ I have never entered into any controversy in defense of my . . . opinions; I leave them to take their chance in the world; if they are *right,* truth and experience will support them; if they are *wrong,* they ought to be repudiated and rejected.

✑ The rapid progress true science now makes, occasions my regretting that I was born so soon.

SCOTLAND

✑ If I had not strong connections draw me elsewhere, I believe Scotland would be the country I should choose to spend the remainder of my days in.

SECRETS

✑ Three may keep a secret if two of them are dead.

⮞ If you would keep your secret from an enemy, tell it not to a friend.

⮞ It is wise not to seek a secret and honest not to reveal it.

SECURITY
⮞ Love your neighbor but don't pull down the hedge.

SEDUCTION
⮞ Neither a fortress or maidenhead will hold out long once they begin to parley.

SELF-INTEREST
⮞ When there is so much to be done for yourself, your family, your country, and your gracious king, be up by the peep of day.

⮞ The noblest question in the world: what good may I do in it?

SELF-RELIANCE
⮞ God helps them that help themselves.

SERVICE
⮞ It has been my opinion that he who receives an estate from his ancestors is under some kind of obligation to transmit the same to their posterity.

SEX
⮞ In your amours you should prefer old women to young ones, they are so grateful!

⚮ Masculine and feminine things (apart from moods and tenses) have been giving me trouble for sixty years. I once hoped that at eighty, I could be delivered, but here I am at four times nineteen {1782} which is very close; nevertheless these French "feminines" still disturb me. This should make me happy to go to paradise, where they say these distinctions are abolished.

SIN
⚮ The most effectual way to get rid of a certain temptation is to comply and satisfy it.

SINCERITY
⚮ The word "Simplicity" is not always meant as Folly or Ignorance; but often [it means] pure and upright nature free from artifice, craft, or deceitful ornament.

SLANDER
⚮ Dirt thrown on a mud-wall may stick but it will not long adhere to polished marble.

⚮ Dunces often write satires on themselves when they think they are mocking their neighbors.

⚮ Splashes of dirt thrown upon my character I suffered, while fresh, to remain. I did not choose to spread by endeavoring to remove them but relied on the vulgar adage that it [excrement] would rub off when it was dry.

SLAVERY

☞ 'Tis an ill-grounded opinion that by the labor of slaves America may possibly vie in cheapness of manufactures with Britain.

☞ Slavery is an atrocious debasement of human nature.

SLEEP

☞ *Early to bed and early to rise,*
Makes a man healthy, wealthy and wise.

SOLITUDE

☞ I acknowledge that solitude is an agreeable refreshment for a busy mind.

SPEAKER

☞ Discourse is often much better than the man—as sweet and clear waters come through a very dirty earth.

STATESMEN

☞ Wise and good men are the strength of a state: much more so than riches or arms.

SUCCESS

☞ Success has ruined many a good man.

TACT

☞ Tell a miser he's rich or a woman she's old and you'll get no money from one nor kindness from the other.

TALENT

 The used key is always bright.

 *Hide not your talents, they for use were made,
What's a sundial in the shade?*

TALK

 The greatest talkers are the least doers.

 He that speaks much is much mistaken.

 Well done is better than well said.

 Words may show a man's wit but actions his meaning.

 You may talk too much on the best of subjects.

TARIFFS

 Therefore what you get from us in taxes you lose in trade.

TAXES

 Nothing is certain but death and taxes.

 That compelling the Colonies to pay money without their consent . . . would be treating them as conquered people and not as true British subjects.

 That it is supposed an undoubted right of Englishmen not to be taxed but by their own consent given through their representatives.

 That by claiming a right to tax us *ad libitum,* they deprived us of all property.

TEACHER

∽ Talents for the education of youth are a gift of God.

TEASING

∽ Joke went out and brought home his fellow and the two began a quarrel.

∽ Thou can'st not joke an enemy into a friend, but thou mayst a friend into an enemy.

TEMPERANCE

∽ Eat not to dullness; drink not to elevation.

TERM LIMITATION

∽ In free governments the rulers are the servants and the people their superiors and sovereigns. For the former, therefore, to return among the latter is not to *degrade* but to *promote* them.

THEOLOGY

∽ Many a long dispute among divines may be thus abridged: It is so, it is not so. It is so, it is not so.

THRIFT

∽ A shilling spent idly by a fool may be picked up by a wiser person.

∽ Spare and have is better than spend and crave.

∽ A prudent wife—if she does not bring a fortune—will make one.

TIME

◦ Remember that time is money.

◦ Since thou are not sure of a minute, throw not away an hour.

◦ Lose no time; be always employed in something useful, cut off all unnecessary actions.

TRADE

◦ No nation was ever ruined by trade, even seemingly the most disadvantageous.

◦ A must take some of B's product, otherwise B will not be able to pay for what he would take of A.

TRAVEL

◦ A traveler should have a hog's nose, deer's legs, and an ass's back.

◦ Traveling is one way of lengthening life, at least in appearance.

TREASON

◦ Prosecution for treason [is] generally virulent and perjury too easily made against innocence.

TRUTH

◦ Endeavor to speak truth in every instance and give nobody expectation that is not likely to be answered, but aim at sincerity in every word and action.

TURKEY

❧ I wish the Bald Eagle had not been chosen as the representative of our country; he is a bird of bad moral character; he does not get his living honestly . . . like those men who live by sharping and robbing, he is generally poor and often very lousy.

TYRANNY

❧ Free government stands on opinion—not on the brutal force of a standing army.

❧ I have held up a Looking Glass in which some Ministers may see their ugly faces and the Nation its Injustice.[24]

❧ When complaining becomes a crime, hope becomes despair.

❧ Rebellion to tyranny is obedience to God.[25]

❧ Are all those subjects rebels who oppose the illegal and oppressive proceedings of lawful government? If this doctrine is orthodox, down goes the [colonies'] revolution and we are all rebels, the Jacobites only excepted, for the Stuarts were lawful sovereigns.

❧ Force sits upon reason's back.

URGENCY

❧ Take time by the forelock.

---

[24] Franklin was describing his role as colonial agent in London.

[25] Franklin chose these words for the U.S. Seal under the Articles of Confederation.

UTOPIA

☙ A future state in which all that appears to be wrong shall be set right, all that is crooked made straight.

VANITY

☙ Vanity backbites more than malice.

☙ Most people dislike vanity in others, whatever share they may have of it themselves.

☙ Three things are men most likely to be cheated in: a horse, a wig, and a wife.

VENEREAL DISEASE

☙ Against diseases, here the strongest fence is the defensive virtue—abstinence.

VICE

☙ A benevolent man should allow a few faults in himself to keep his friends in countenance.

☙ What maintains one vice would bring up two children.

☙ Let thy vices die before thee.

☙ Man thinks he's buying pleasure when he is really making himself a slave to it.

VIRTUE

☙ But what is Wit or Wealth or Form [fashion or style] or Learning when compared to Virtue?

VISIONARY

☞ The eye of the master will do more than both his hands.

☞ *Today the statesman of new honor dreams*
tomorrow death destroys his airy schemes.

VISITORS

☞ The busy man has few idle visitors; to the boiling pot the flies come not.

☞ Fish and visitors stink after three days.

VOCATION

☞ He that hath a trade hath an estate.

☞ The man who lives by his labor is at least free.

WAGES

☞ A law might be made to raise wages but if our manufacturers are too dear, they will not vend abroad and all part of that employment will fail.

WAR

☞ It is remarkable that soldiers by profession, men truly and unquestionably brave, seldom advise war but in cases of extreme necessity.

☞ What vast additions to the convenience and comforts of living might Mankind have acquired if the money spent in wars had been employed in public utility.

∞ I believe in my conscience that Mankind is wicked enough to continue slaughtering one another as long as they can find enough money to pay the butchers.

∞ War are all follies, with little or no advantage gained even by those who win temporarily. But useful ideas are deathless and permanent—they shape the true progress of mankind.

∞ Men seem to take more pride and even pleasure in killing than in begetting one another. For without a blush they assemble in great armies as they can to destroy and when they have killed as many as they can, they exaggerate the number to augment the fancied glory.

WAR FOR INDEPENDENCE
∞ We are fighting for the dignity and happiness of human nature. Glorious is it for the American to be called by Providence to this post of honor.

∞ Our cause is the cause of all mankind, and . . . we are fighting for their liberty in defending our own.

WASTREL
∞ The prodigal generally does more injustice than the covetous.

WEAKNESS
∞ Make yourselves sheep and the wolves will eat you.

WEALTH
∞ In death there is no difference between dying worth a great sum and dying in debt for a great sum.

⁂ *A rich rogue is like a fat hog*
Who never does any good 'til he's dead as a log.

WEATHERMAN

⁂ Although it was I who made the almanac, the Lord God made the weather.

WENCHING

⁂ After three days men grow weary of a wench, a guest, and weather rainy.

WIDOWS

⁂ Rich widows are the only second-hand goods that sell at first-class prices.

WIFE

⁂ You can bear your own faults. Why not a fault in your wife?

⁂ I know not which live more unnatural lives, obeying husbands or commanding wives.

⁂ Women who smart under the tyranny of a bad husband ought to be fixed in revolution principles.

⁂ A house without a woman and firelight is like a body without soul or spirit.

⁂ A good wife and health is man's best wealth.

⁂ He that must thrive must ask his wife.

⁂ A man without a wife is but half a man.

∞ *You cannot pluck roses without danger of thorns*
   Nor enjoy a fair wife without danger of horns {being cuckolded}.

WISDOM

∞ He is a fool that cannot conceal his wisdom.

∞ That none but the virtuous are wise.

∞ The doors of wisdom are never shut.

WISHES

∞ If a man could have half his wishes, he would double his troubles.

WIT

∞ There's many witty men whose brains can't fill their bellies.

WOMEN

∞ If knowledge and understanding had been useless additions to the sex, God Almighty would never have given them capacities, for He made nothing needless.

∞ When women cease to be handsome, they study to be good.

∞ The proof of gold is fire, the proof of woman gold: the proof of a man, a woman.

∞ Let the fair sex be assured that I shall always treat them in their affairs with the utmost decency and respect.

WORRY

❦ Be not disturbed at trifles or at accidents common or unavoidable.

YOUTH

❦ Virtue and a trade are a child's best portion.

❦ If this season [time of education] is neglected, it will be like cutting off Spring from the year.

❦ Teach your child to hold his tongue, he'll learn fast enough to speak.

❦ *Youth is pert and positive. Age modest and doubting.*
   So ears of corn when young and light stand bolt upright but
   hang their heads when weighty full and ripe.

Franklin Firsts

Time, place, and man all converged when Benjamin Franklin came to Philadelphia in 1723. For a newly emerging city in a new century, Franklin was a new kind of thinker.

It was the beginning of the eighteenth century—which historians called the Age of Enlightenment—when new ideas about the infinite possibilities of man would shatter the dark theological doctrines of man's inherent evil. To think that man was perfectible was a blasphemous opinion when Franklin was a boy in Boston.

When Franklin arrived in Philadelphia, he left the Puritan dogma behind in Boston. To the natural optimism of youth, he also brought a curious nature and inventive mind.

Philadelphia was not Puritan, but Quaker. The Society of Friends rejected a formal theology: Divine instruction was to come from within—from an inner light. Franklin never joined the Society, but his own ideas of self-improvement found a congenial climate.

When Philadelphia (the "City of Brotherly Love" in Greek) was being named and laid out by William Penn in 1682, Boston was the biggest population center of the English colonies. After all, it was the closest colonial seaport to London.

William Penn's Commonwealth hung out its "open door" sign to all religious pilgrims—Scotch Presbyterians, Moravian Anabaptists, French Huguenots, German Lutherans, and Palatinate followers of Jacob Mennon, who were the plainly clothed Mennonites and Amish. All these seekers for a land where they could practice their faith arrived at the Philadelphia docks. As a result, the settlement that was Philadelphia quickly grew from a town into a small city.

By the 1740s the population of Philadelphia exceeded that of Boston to become, next to London, the biggest city in the British Empire. Such a metropolis-to-be had the growing pains of unmet needs—urban services such as police and fire protection, medical requirements such as a hospital, and demands for educational facilities such as schools and a library.

Philadelphia was fortunate to have in its midst a young energetic printer and shopkeeper with the vision to foresee those needs. Franklin, who is now recognized as the embodiment of the Age of Enlightenment, was a can-do optimist, a born promoter, and an indefatigable civic booster. Mr. Franklin was a "Mr. Fix-It." He was the right man, in the right place, at the right time.

❧ ❧ ❧

ABOLITION OF SLAVERY

In 1787 Franklin organized the first abolition society in America, becoming its president. He rejected the idea that blacks were innately inferior, saying that they were victims of their environment and of a deprived education. In the last public act of his life, Franklin, in 1789, would sign a Memorial to the newly assembled U.S. House of Representatives to abolish the slave trade. Yet privately Franklin voiced the sad prophecy that only a civil war would end slavery in America.

AIR POLLUTION CONTROL

In a letter in 1744, Franklin denounced the danger of sulfurous smoke, saying, "When so much less of that smoke shall be made, the air breathed by the inhabitants will be consequently so much purer." Franklin recommended the curtailment of chimney smoke.

AUTOBIOGRAPHY

Franklin was not the first American to write his memoirs, but his was the first to be a commercial success, the equivalent of today's bestseller. It was even translated in his day into French, German, and Spanish. Although the first edition came out when he was thirty-seven, he published subsequent updated versions until a few years before his death.

BATHTUB

Franklin imported the first bathtub to America to be installed in his Philadelphia house. It was a French model made of copper, and was shaped like a slipper. Franklin was also a pioneer of indoor plumbing in America.

BIBLE (MODERN-LANGUAGE)

Franklin proposed the translation of the Bible into conversational English. He even wrote out various passages to prove his idea.

BROOM CROP

Franklin introduced broom corn into this country. The dried and treated stalks of the European variety of corn were used to make the broom. Franklin experimented with the first crop of broom corn in New Jersey, which led to the start of the broom industry in America.

EDITORIAL

Franklin introduced the editorial to the pages of his Pennsylvania *Gazette*. It consisted of either Franklin's or the editor's opinion on current political issues. It was decades before other American newspapers followed suit.

EMBASSY

The first U.S. Embassy abroad was established by Franklin in 1777 when he was deputized by the Continental Congress to be the U.S. minister to France. Franklin set up the U.S. Diplomatic Mission in Versailles, home of the court of Louis XVI.

FIRE DEPARTMENT

When Franklin organized the Philadelphia Fire Department, it was the first of its kind in Philadelphia. Originally it was formed on cooperative principles as part of a fire insurance mutual.

The price of admittance for coverage to house-owners was an ax. The new member had then to volunteer his services as a fireman. Monthly meetings were required. Absences incurred fines. The fine money amassed was used to purchase a wagon and hose. Those with the sign of the insurance company on their home were entitled to priority attention by the fire company.

Later, as the company of wagons, horses, and hoses took shape, Franklin separated it from the Insurance Society and established a city department.

FOUNDATION

In his will Franklin created two trusts of a thousand British pounds—each for the two cities that shaped his life. For his native city of Boston he created the Franklin Fund to award a silver medal prize to the top student of Boston Latin, a Boston academy that accepted male students from all classes of society.

For his adopted city of Philadelphia he established the Philadelphia Trust, interest from which would be used to pay for an education in a vocation or trade for students from poor and needy families.

FRANCHISING

Although Franklin did not use the word, he was the first to develop what has now become a familiar corporate device. He would finance an employee in his printing shop to establish the employee's own store. Franklin would supply newsprint, stationery, books, and almanacs. The franchises would in turn pay Franklin back a third of their profits. Through Franklin's backing, shops were set up in Charleston, South Carolina; the West Indies; New York City; and other places.

HOSPITAL

Franklin professed to disdain doctors. Nevertheless, he helped establish the first American hospital. With his friend Dr. Thomas Bond he set up Pennsylvania Hospital in 1752. Today it still serves Philadelphia residents. Actually the Pennsylvania Assembly originally balked at the size of the appropriation. So Franklin negotiated a compromise. If private citizens raised in subscription half the money needed, the Assembly would then match it with the other half. Franklin also drew up plans for the first medical school in 1790.

INDOOR PLUMBING

Franklin designed the first second-story toilet for his Philadelphia house. The commode with pipes was directly situated over the toilet on the first floor.

INSURANCE SOCIETY

The first insurance company in America was a mutual, for fire and casualty. Franklin conceived the idea when a neighbor's house burned down. He then proposed a pooling together of funds for insurance purposes.

LENDING LIBRARY

As a young printer in Philadelphia, Franklin proposed to his bibliophile friends that each donate several books to a library. The pooled collection became a mutual library. Fines for overdrawn books were used to buy new books.

Soon Franklin opened it up to the public and he named it the Free Library, in contrast to the libraries of universities or private libraries such as the Athenaeum later established in Philadelphia. Franklin's lending library is still called the Free Library.

Some of the early books the Free Library ordered from England included the *Iliad*, the *Odyssey*, Dryden's translation of Virgil, Plutarch's *Lives*, and the *Annals of Tacitus*.

NAVY

When the War for Independence began, American ports lay helpless against the British navy. Although the colonies could never hope to drive the British fleet from American shores, Franklin believed a few commissioned vessels might make the British sea war costly. He commandeered three merchant cutters into action—the *Black Prince*, the *Black Princess*, and the *Fearnot*—and gave their captains commissions from the Continental Congress to foray against the British ships. Such was the beginning of the American navy.

NOVEL

Franklin did not write the first novel in America, but he did publish the first. Samuel Richardson's *Pamela*—probably the first English-language novel—was published in London in 1742. In 1744 Franklin published it in America.

PHILOSOPHICAL SOCIETY

At age thirty-six Franklin organized the American Philosophical Society in 1743. Because of his age and lack of formal education he let more venerable academics serve as president in the first years, reserving for himself the title of secretary. The society, which was scientific as well as philosophical in study, was the oldest of its kind in America. It was modeled after the Royal Society in Britain. The Philosophical Society published reports and heard lectures at its meetings.

In 1767 he would become its president. Subsequent presidents would include David Rittenhouse and Thomas Jefferson.

POLITICAL CARTOON

Franklin drew the first political cartoon published in America. As the French and Indian War loomed, Franklin proposed a union of the colonies at the Congress in Albany, New York, in 1754.

To dramatize the need for unity, he sketched a snake carved up in thirteen bits (identifying the pieces as each of the colonies), and underneath the snake was the slogan "Unite or Die." The widespread popularity of the published cartoon led to the "Don't Tread on Me" Flag raised by rebelling colonists twenty years later.

SERVICE CLUB

Franklin founded the Junto—a club which may be said to be a forerunner of the Rotary, Kiwanis, Lions, and other businessmen's clubs today. The ostensible aims were self-improvement and fellowship, yet the underlying purpose of the different tradesmen and craftsmen who met weekly was networking—developing contacts that would help each other's business or trade. One motto was, "Do you think of anything at present in which the Junto may be serviceable to *mankind* or to themselves?"

SUBSCRIPTION CONTEST

To increase subscriptions for the *Gazette* newspaper as well as his almanac, Franklin offered prizes of free subscriptions to those who could answer riddles and games. He even invited readers to write a letter of a hundred words or less—or sometimes a short poem:

Who shall in good verse explain me clear
Shall have this Gazette *free, one year.*

TRADE CATALOG

In 1744 Franklin published the first trade catalog in America. It was a list of books Franklin was offering for sale by mail.

VERTICAL MONOPOLY

Franklin may not have known the term, but he understood its economic advantage. When demand made prices of newsprint soar, he built his own paper mill to give him a constant and cheaper supply. He then could undercut his competitors.

WINDSURFING

Franklin was the first to enjoy the sport of windsurfing. First he employed kites to propel him while floating in a lake. Then he used the kites for a raft.

Inventions, Ideas, and Discoveries

Franklin was a printer by vocation. His avocation, however, was science. He had started out as a printer and quickly moved into publishing—first as the owner of the Pennsylvania *Gazette* and then the almanac. By his mid-forties he had made enough money to retire from printing and turn to his first love—science.

To Franklin, science was nature—physical and human nature. It was as if he wanted to interrogate Mother Nature for her secrets. If curiosity is a quality of youth, Franklin never aged. Life for him was a continuing laboratory in which he sought the answers of life.

As a young man returning west from London to Philadelphia, he had to know why it took a longer time than crossing eastward. That curiosity would eventually lead to his discovery of the Gulf Stream.

Lightning and its strikes tore at Franklin's mind. His famous experiment using the kite and key was the basis of the first published reports that proved that electricity existed in lightning. It was those findings that first brought Franklin recognition in Europe.

A true representative of the Age of Enlightenment, Franklin did not unquestioningly accept the dogma of the past.

For example, in Franklin's day, physicians shut up the sick in closed rooms. Franklin attacked that practice. He proposed opening the windows to let in the light and sunshine. That belief, contrary to the prevailing wisdom of the day, may be a metaphor to describe his curious and inquiring mind. Let the light of experiment and truths, said Franklin, be applied to ignorant prejudices.

What if new findings challenged his beliefs? asked a friend. Would he fight for his beliefs? Franklin shook his head. To Franklin, one had to expose one's beliefs to truth and not try to cover up. He applied that principle to personal hygiene. He championed nudism or, as he called it, "air bathing."

His belief in truth led him to forgo applying for patents for his inventions such as the lightning rod. Truth, said Franklin, belonged to mankind and not one man. So, believing that ideas, inventions, and discoveries that better the condition of mankind should be free, Franklin would accept no profit.

In his Philadelphia workshop his puttering was suggestive of the contemporary American man whose favorite Father's Day gifts come from the hardware store. Among other devices Franklin fashioned for himself was an "artificial arm" with pincers to retrieve books high on a shelf. For the same purpose he crafted a library chair with steps stored under the seat for reaching high shelves. Franklin's favorite chair was one of the rocking variety that operated, with foot pedals, a fan that not only kept one cool but also kept the flies away.

Yet his interests encompassed far more than the comforts of home. In the Junto—the club he organized that was the forerunner of the modern Rotary and Kiwanis clubs—he called for the sponsoring of a trek to investigate the North Pole. The trip was aborted, but Franklin did investigate the causes of the aurora borealis.

Franklin never lost the curiosity of youth. At age seventy-six he watched in Paris the ascent of air balloons and foresaw the possibilities of air travel. He said a few years before his death that he wished he could live in the twentieth century. He would have been quite at home in this technological era.

≈ ≈ ≈

AIR FORCE

While in France, Franklin observed the balloon flight of Joseph-Michel Montgolfier in Paris. From his French home in Passy, then a suburb of Paris, Franklin wrote, "Man may be supported in air—nothing is wanted but some light handy instruments to give and direct motion."

Franklin foresaw the use of balloons or other craft to carry troops and weapons in war. Noting how impossible it would be to defend against an invasion of troops by air, Franklin foresaw how troops could be "descending from the clouds before a force could be brought together to repel them."

ALPHABET

Franklin proposed a new alphabet of only twenty letters, including six new ones he devised to denote such sounds as *th* and *zh* (as in *pleasure*).

Some of the letters he eliminated were *Q, X, Y,* and *K* (the *C* would only be a hard *C,* as in *cut*). (See the figure opposite, which was taken from Volume 15 of *The Papers of Benjamin Franklin* [1972].)

Characters.	Sounded as now in ⌐	Names of the Letters, expres'd in the reformed Sounds and Characters	
o	old	o	the first Vowel naturally, and deepest sound; requires only to open the Mouth, and breathe thro' it.
a[o]¹	John, Folly	a	the next, requiring the Mouth open'd a little more, or hollower.
a	man, can	a	the next, a little more.
e	mane, lane	e	the next, requires the Tongue to be a little more elevated } tho the Pipe above will form them, but not so easily.
i	een, seen	i	the next, still a little more.
u	tool, fool	u	the next, requires the Lips to be gather'd up, leaving a small Opening.
y[y; Y]¹	um, un, as in umbrage, unto, &c.	y	the next, a very short Vowel, the Sound of which we should express in our present Letters thus, uh, short and not very strong Aspiration.
h	hunter, happy, high	huh	a stronger or more forcible Aspiration.
g	give, gather	gi	the first Consonant, being form'd by the Root of the Tongue, this is the present hard g.
k	keep, kick	ki	a blunted Sound, a little more acute, so be us'd instead of the hard c.
s[ʃ]¹	sh, ship, wish	ish	a new Letter, wanted in our Language, our sh, separately taken, not being proper Elements of the Sound.
ŋ [ɳ]¹	ng, ing, reaping, among	ing	a new Letter, wanted for the same Reason; these are form'd back in the Mouth.
n	end	en	form'd more forward in the Mouth, the Tip of the Tongue to the Roof of the Mouth.
r	art	ar	the more, the Tip of the Tongue a little loose or separate from the Roof of the Mouth.
t	teeth	ti	the Tip of the Tongue more forward, touching and then leaving the Roof.
d	deed	di	the same, touching a little fuller.
l	ell, tell	el	the same, touching just about the Gums of the upper Teeth.
đ [ð, Ď]¹	dh, thy	eth	the Tongue under and a little behind the upper Teeth, touching them nearly but so as to let the Breath pass between.
s	essence	es	the same a little fuller.
z	ez, wages	ez	this Sound is form'd by the Breath passing between the moist End of the Tongue and the upper Teeth.
f	effect	ef	the more a little denser and duller.
v	ever	ev	form'd by the lower Lip against the upper Teeth.
b	bees	bi	the same fuller and duller.
p	peep	pi	the lips put full together and open'd as the Air passes out.
m	ember	em	the same but a thinner Sound. the closing of the Lips, while the e is sounding.

1. For the six new letters proposed by me, both comma and italic lower case characters have been cut based on his designs (see note 3 above, p. 179). Franklin also made designs for all six capitals, but only the two that occur in the texts printed in this volume have been cut.

From Leonard Labaree et al., eds., *The Papers of Benjamin Franklin,* Volume 15, opposite p. 179. Reprinted with permission.

ARMONICA

Although Franklin enjoyed the music of Handel, his true tastes ran to ballads of the day. His contribution to music was his invention of the "armonica." It was in France, while serving as envoy, that Franklin invented this musical instrument which was an adaption of sets of tuned glasses, and which the musician sat before as a piano or organ. Both Mozart and Beethoven composed for the armonica.

ARTIFICIAL ARM

The printing shop Franklin owned and ran with his wife started with selling printing supplies but soon expanded to include stationery, pens, ink, candles, and books. Shelves reaching to the ceiling soon had to be built to store all the supplies. To obviate the use of a stepladder, the practical Franklin invented an "artificial arm"—a hook with pincers on a long stick that would grasp the item. He soon was selling the pincered arm out of his shop. He also kept another "artificial arm" in his library to reach books on the top shelves.

BIFOCALS

Although the word *bifocals* did not appear in print until the 1890s, Franklin did invent them. Franklin, however, used the term "double spectacles."

At the time of the treaty negotiation for concluding the Revolutionary War in France in 1782, Franklin had to carry two pairs of glasses—one for reading, and one for everyday living. So he designed his "double spectacles" and took them to a lensmaker in Paris.

He wrote of telling French lensmakers to have "the glasses cut and half of each lens in the same circle. By this means—as I wear my spectacles constantly—I have only to move my eyes up and down, as I want to see distinctly far or near."

CATHETER

Franklin was responsible for the first catheter in American medicine. His brother John in Boston had a urinary ailment and asked for Franklin's advice. Franklin suggested the use of lime water and soap and then devised the catheter, made of pewter. Franklin himself went to a silversmith's and gave directions on how to make it. Franklin then supervised the making of it.

CLOCK (*With a Hand for Seconds*)

Franklin was the first—at least in this country—to devise a clock with three wheels showing hours, minutes, and seconds.

COMPARTMENTALIZED UNITS ON SHIPS

Franklin was among the first to recommend that sailing vessels be constructed with sealed units as a safety measure. Such compartmentalized rooms and storage units, he asserted, would reduce the risk of the ship foundering quickly at sea.

CONTINENTAL DRIFT

In 1782 Franklin discovered oyster shells at the foot of a mountain in England. From that he deduced the geological shifts of ocean and landmass.

DAYLIGHT SAVINGS TIME

As publisher of America's favorite almanac, Franklin printed in calendars the times of the sun rising and setting. Since farmers worked from sunup to sundown, why, asked Franklin, should city shops and offices be closed in the early morning hours of the summer? Accordingly he proposed a "Daylight Savings Time." It would not be adopted until a century and a half later in 1918 during World War I.

DEAD LETTER OFFICE

As postmaster general for the American colonies, Franklin noted that letters misdirected or unreceived were thrown away. Accordingly, he conceived of a "dead letter office" to store those letters so they would be available for further inquiry. In a day when mail traffic was relatively light, worried correspondents could apply to the dead letter office of their town.

DESALINIZATION

Franklin came up with a unique way of taking salt out of seawater. While on ships he observed that the human body, with its porous tissue, absorbs the salt while bathing in ocean water. So Franklin proposed that as an emergency measure, sailors take water they had soaked in and afterward boil the water to be later used as drinking water.

DISASTER RELIEF

Franklin proposed setting up an office to administer aid to farmers whose crops had been destroyed by hurricanes, tornadoes, blights, or pestilence. An office could collect a small premium for insurance and then inspect the damage for payment.

ELECTRICITY IN LIGHTNING

Franklin did not discover electricity, but he did prove that electricity existed in lightning. The tale of Franklin with kite and key is part of our American legend. His experiment, however, was highly dangerous. A Belgian scientist some years earlier had been electrocuted by a similar test.

Because the churches in Quaker Philadelphia were steepleless, Franklin had his son fly a kite, which he knew—at the highest point—would attract lightning during a storm. A string attached to the kite held a metal key. Franklin, to insulate himself, did not grasp the key in his hand, but held a Leyden jar that contained the key. When lightning struck the kite, a spark ignited in the jar, proving his hypothesis. He published the results of the experiment in the *Gazette,* and it was reported in scientific journals abroad.

EUROPEAN COMMUNITY

Franklin was among the first to propose a European federation. In 1787 he sent to European friends a copy of the new U.S. Constitution suggesting that they should "form a federal union of its different states."

FRANKLIN STOVE

Franklin's most useful invention was a stove that could be installed in the fireplace. The stove allowed smoke to rise without taking the heat with it. A device pushed the heat out into the room, radiating a greater warmth throughout the hearth room.

GERM CONTAGION

A century before Louis Pasteur, Franklin voiced the idea that circulation of air could prevent and fight disease. Although physicians in Franklin's time shut up the windows in rooms where sick patients lay, Franklin urged opening them. In letters to medical societies, Franklin explained that airless rooms, filled with people, were both spreaders as well as incubators of germs.

GULF STREAM

As early as 1745, Franklin was pondering why ships sailing from America to England would have quicker voyages than returning ships. Over the next ten years Franklin would ask various ship captains the time differential in their voyage and their reasons for the variance. Some mentioned a kind of current.

Franklin would write in 1767 that a voyager may know when he is in the Gulf Stream by the warmth of the water. Franklin was the first to call this eastward current the "Gulf Stream," and he had a map printed plotting its course.

INFLUENZA AND LIQUIDS

Franklin had a general disdain for most doctors and a contempt for the medicines they prescribed. He preferred to trust in the healing potions of Mother Nature, such as rest and plenty of water. "Liquids (not alcohol!) and sleep" was his medicine for the common cold and influenza—a regimen which today's doctors prescribe.

INFRASTRUCTURE

Franklin never knew the word, but he observed in his life the unfortunate trend of governments to build the new before repairing the old. In his will he left money to the city of Philadelphia earmarked for the repair of bridges, roads, and public buildings two hundred years after his death.

LETTER COPIER
Using a rolling press, Franklin fashioned a device that would make copies of the letters he had penned.

LIBRARY CHAIR
Franklin delighted in showing visitors the library chair he built. The seat of his chair could be pulled up to reveal steps that one could mount to retrieve books on a high shelf.

LIGHTNING ROD
After Franklin's kite experiment, he pondered how to protect houses from being struck by lightning. To prevent the fire hazard, Franklin proposed that a rod on the roof be connected to "a wire down outside the building into the ground." For a rod on a ship, he said, the wire could extend into the sea.

MATCHED GIVING
Franklin was America's first champion fund-raiser. He solicited money for hospitals, schools, and universities.

It was Franklin who came up with the idea of the "matched gift" device. When Franklin's appropriation bill to establish a hospital in Philadelphia was rejected by the Pennsylvania General Assembly, he rewrote the bill for half the appropriation, conditional on raising the other half by voluntary public subscription.

He would later use the matched-gift plan to leverage large gifts from rich donors or to spur would-be small donors to achieve a fund goal.

NUDISM

Franklin championed what he called "air bathing"—the exposure of the nude body to the sun. He had the habit of sitting nude in a sun-filled room reading his books.

PENAL REFORM

Franklin was the first American to advocate reform in the prison system. He doubted the long-term effects of whipping and other forms of corporal punishment. One of his contributions in his long career of public service was to lobby for graduated terms of prison sentences for crimes against the state, to be decided by the presiding judge. In 1789, Pennsylvania was the first state to introduce terms of sentences to fit the crime.

PHYSICAL FITNESS

Franklin's advice for fitness and good health are echoed by every doctor today as a prescription to prevent hypertension and disease of the heart. His test was not the amount of exercise but the raising of the pulse rate. His recommendations included a brisk walk, climbing up stairs, and the use of barbells as a daily regimen to strengthen the heart.

PLANETARY LIFE

Franklin believed that life on other planets was not improbable. He held that "space is in every way infinite" and that a "chorus of worlds with suns like ours" had their own movement and forms of life.

REFLECTION OF HEAT

Franklin tried to popularize the idea of wearing light clothes in summer, which would reflect the sun's heat. Dark attire, on the other hand, he counseled, absorbed the sun's heat rays.

SECURITY MIRROR

Franklin devised a mirror that would reveal who was at the front door before it was opened. The invention, called the "Philadelphia Busybody," was a double set of mirrors—a reflecting mirror from the second story, which was then picked up by another mirror on the first floor.

"SOAP OPERA" SERIAL

Two centuries before comic strips or radio soap operas were ever seen or heard, Franklin came up with the idea of a continuing comic narration of a conjugal couple that would suggest the *Blondie* sitcom of this century.

To add spice and reader interest to his almanac, Franklin would intersperse the pages not only with sayings of Poor Richard, but also with the marital vicissitudes of Richard's life. Richard Saunders was a plodding Quaker astronomer with a shrewish wife named Bridget. The humorous antics of the domestic duo made Franklin's almanac the most successful American publication of his day. In 1732 it was the first to be sold outside of its own colony. Eventually it would be popular in all thirteen colonies. Its total yearly sales would be a half million.

SHOCK TREATMENTS

From his studies and experiments with electricity, Franklin proposed that electric jolts might be therapeutic with the mentally ill. After noting the calming effects of light shocks on dogs and turkeys, Franklin wrote papers on the possible salutary effects on mental patients.

STREET LIGHTING

Although Franklin did not introduce streetlights, he did invent a four-sided ventilated street lamp that replaced the old English globe. The Franklin lamp not only emitted less smoke, but burned less fuel. Before Franklin, the London lamps offered only a hazy glow that was more smoke than light. Franklin's invention gave better light to the streets of Philadelphia, thereby rendering them more safe.

SUBMARINE

In 1776 Franklin invited David Bushnell to come to Philadelphia. Franklin was fascinated with Bushnell's submarine. Bushnell called it the *Turtle*. In Delaware Bay, the *Turtle* under ocean level propelled a bomb toward a British flagship of Admiral Howe's. The attempt was unsuccessful, but Franklin was not dissuaded from the idea of a submarine's use in future wars.

VITAMIN C

Centuries before Vitamin C was discovered and identified, Franklin championed the eating of citrus fruits such as oranges, limes, and grapefruits. His favorite food was the apple. The phrase "An apple a day keeps the doctor away" was his advice. "Fruit," said

Franklin, "is essential for maintaining gums and skin." It was not until 1795—years after Franklin's published recommendations—that the British navy put a lime in the daily British seaman's ration. After that, "limey" became a popular synonym for an Englishman.

Franklin Fables

The perception of the real Ben Franklin is obscured by the caricature. Just as Winston Churchill is sometimes pictured as a drunk who was rude to women, Franklin is often seen as an old lecher.

Perhaps no other historical personality in America is beset by such conflicting images—penny-pinching shopkeeper, flier of the kite, coiner of maxims, tinkering inventor, wise statesman. Franklin had more energy—including sexual—but America's first feminist cannot be labeled a "dirty old man."

In a sense, Franklin opened himself up for criticism when he created, for the pages of his almanac, the character of Poor Richard, the Quaker polymath and weatherman. For Poor Richard was the oracle for all Franklin's homilies for good behavior.

Poor Richard urged chastity, yet the real Franklin fathered a child out of wedlock. Poor Richard counseled fidelity, yet Franklin strayed from those vows in London while serving as the agent for the American colonies. Poor Richard preached humility, yet Franklin—though careful to affect modesty in public—was a master of self-promotion. Still, Franklin was no "colonial Casanova." If he did have scores of affairs, he was successful in hiding them from historical scrutiny.

His foes called him not only an amorist but an atheist. He was not. He was a deist like Thomas Jefferson, who was a Unitarian. Deists such as Franklin believed in God as the Creator but rejected such theological doctrines as the "Trinity" and "Salvation." Yet it should be remembered that it was Franklin who offered the motion at the Constitutional Convention that the proceedings be opened with prayer.

When Franklin was the colonial agent in London before the Revolutionary War, his foes in Philadelphia circulated rumors that he was a Tory about to be knighted by King George III for his connivance with British ministers. True, Franklin praised the young king upon his accession to the throne. Most Americans joined him. Franklin and most of the other colonials believed they were Englishmen and zealously guarded their rights as Englishmen. Franklin would have happily settled for a home rule or dominion status for the American colonies. In this, Franklin reflected the consensus of most Americans.

Franklin's foes also wondered if he was really only the simple printer he always would announce himself to be. Or was this a public relations posture that would allow him to be all the more lionized by French intellectuals and nobility? Under a simple guise Franklin concealed contradictory elements and a complicated nature. Outwardly he played to the hilt the role of American to Europe—an exaggerated prototype that fit the idealized perception of the best of the New World. Yet this "first American" was also his country's first citizen of the world. Conversant in several languages, the "simple" Franklin was in fact a cosmopolite who enjoyed the company of the world's elite.

ๆ ๆ ๆ

ADVISE AND DISSENT
When the Constitutional Convention finished drafting the document, it was, at best, a compromise or consensus that was far from unanimous. A statement that voiced a minority report was likely.

Franklin thought that published dissent on various provisions would make ratification all the more difficult.

At the close of the convention Franklin shrewdly proposed that the delegates merely sign their presence, which did not connote endorsement. In that way, Franklin suggested, the appearance of dissent would be muted and appear unanimous.

THE BALANCE SHEET
Franklin was venerated for his Solomonic wisdom. Self-discipline curbed any half-baked comments from Franklin. He preferred not to utter views on controversial topics until he had time to deliberate privately. His practice was to write down reasons pro and con for adopting a course of action. He counseled readers to emulate the practice. He added that readers might want to assess the weight of each reason—giving some double impact so that one double-weighted reason for could cancel out two single-weighted reasons against.

BEN'S BOO-BOOS

Franklin nourished and promoted the myth of Richard Saunders's existence. Poor Richard in the pages of the almanac would complain of Franklin's sloppy editing.

In my last {issue} a few faults escaped,
some belong to the author {Poor Richard}, but most
to the printer {Franklin} . . .

Printers indeed should be very careful how
they omit a figure or a letter.

Franklin would even have his fictional creation call him stupid. One verse by Poor Richard said:

Ben beats his Pate and fancies wit will come
He may knock, but there's nobody at home.

THE BISHOP TRIP

When Franklin returned from England to Philadelphia in May 1775, the conflict with England had already spilled blood at Concord Bridge the month before.

Worried about its northern border, the Continental Congress proposed to Franklin that he journey to Canada to win over the French-speaking colonists who had been defeated and reduced to a British dominion.

Franklin was not hopeful, but he insisted on taking a priest with him to assure the French that the American colonies were not anti-Catholic. The clergyman he chose was John Carroll of Baltimore, a scion of a distinguished Maryland Catholic family.

The Franklin mission was not fruitful, but it did influence the choice of the first American bishop. At the end of the war, John Carroll was appointed bishop. His friendship with the world-famous Franklin was the reason for his bishopric.

BON AMI

Benjamin Franklin is an American folk hero, but the French also adopted him as hero. As well they should! It was the French-speaking Franklin who suggested the national motto of the French republic, "*Liberté, égalité, fraternité.*"

CAT-ASTROPHE

Franklin often turned to fable to voice his warnings about what would happen if the oppressive tax tyranny of the British continued.

One story he had printed up was about an eagle who sighted from the sky an easy prey—a rabbit.

The eagle swooped and lifted the creature by the neck, only to find that he had picked up not a bunny but a bobcat.

The eagle tried to drop its catch, but the cat put its talons into the eagle's breast. So the wounded eagle had to take the cat back to the very spot where the attack occurred. Then the cat unclenched its claws and walked proudly away.

CLEAN SWEEP

A package from France arrived one day at Franklin's house in Philadelphia. He opened it to find a splendid broom, and he remembered that he admired one like it in his days as envoy to France.

Yet if the donor had expected Franklin to employ his gift for sweeping, he was mistaken. When he saw three seeds on top of the stalks, he determined that sowing, not sweeping, would be the outcome of this particular broom.

The pellets on top of the stems were seeds of the broom plant. In this way Franklin introduced the broom crop and broom industry to America!

"DOCTOR DROPOUT"

To the world, the "Sage of Philadelphia" was known as Dr. Franklin. He had received doctorate degrees from America's three oldest universities: Harvard, William and Mary, and Yale.

Across the Atlantic, Oxford as well as two Scottish institutions of learning, the University of Edinburgh and the University of St. Andrew's, also conferred on him a doctorate of laws.

Yet Franklin had only two years of schooling. He left school at nine—first to work for his father in a candle shop, then to apprentice for his brother James, the printer. The "doctor" had been a dropout!

EAGER BEAVERS

When Franklin appeared at the Court of Versailles to present his credentials as minister, he created a sensation with his attire. No silk, no ruffles, and no velvet for Franklin, and even no wig.

He, did, however, cover his balding head with a round fur hat made of beaver skin.

The beaver hat soon became the rage for French ladies of fashion. They pressed their milliners to order furs and devise for them "*le chapeau à la Franklin.*"

EDITING GOD?

Franklin was never shy about taking on the theologians of his day. His efforts to rewrite parts of the Bible were, in the eyes of the clerics, his most flagrant act of apostasy.

Although the King James version of the Bible was not even a century and a half old, it had become more than the Bible, it was "God's word." To amend it was to edit God. Here is a sample of Franklin's rewrite of Job.

KING JAMES VERSION	FRANKLIN'S VERSION
7. And the Lord said unto Satan, "Whence cometh thou?" Then Satan answered the Lord and said, "From going to and fro in the earth and from walking up and down it."	7. And God said to Satan, "You have been some time absent, where were you?" And Satan answered, "I have been at my county seat and different places visiting my friends."
8. And the Lord said unto Satan, "Hast thou considered my servant Job, that there is none like him in the earth, a perfect and an upright man, one that feareth God and escheweth evil?"	8. And God said, "Well, what think you of Lord Job? You see he is my best friend, a perfectly honest man. Full of respect for me and avoiding everything that might offend me."

FAT CATS FIRST!

Franklin was America's first successful fund-raiser. His reputation led many to ask Franklin to solicit contributions for their own particular cause. Once a minister sought Franklin to raise money for the building of a new church. Franklin demurred. Why, thought Franklin, should he wear out his welcome with rich citizens by constantly dunning them? The preacher then asked Franklin to give him a list of Philadelphia's most generous givers. Franklin again refused, but agreed to give his method for solicitation. The formula is still used by charitable groups today.

"Make three lists," counseled Franklin. "First those who are most likely to give. Second, those who may or may not give, and third those who, in all probability, will not give at all."

"Then," said Franklin, "use those who give in the first list as leverage for those in the second list."

"Finally," added Franklin, "go to those in the third list armed with the names of those givers in the first two lists who are close friends or associates of those in the third list."

FEMINIST OR WOMANIZER?

There is some evidence to support both claims. Of course, the words are not mutually exclusive. In today's U.S. Senate some of the most ardent advocates of women's rights have been philanderers.

By eighteenth-century standards, Franklin was a feminist before the word was known. At age seventeen in "The Silence Dogood Letters," Franklin shocked Puritan Boston with the notion that women might be able to manage shops, preach sermons, and read law better than men.

Still, the sexist comments expressed by his fictional character Poor Richard were in the chauvinist spirit of the times. One thing is certain: Franklin respected the intelligence of women when few in his day did. He took seriously women's opinions when others only indulged them.

That singular quality—along with his sense of humor—
endeared him to women. Women, it is said, judge by what they hear,
while men judge by what they see. Franklin was no Adonis. When
he lived in London and Paris—the scenes of most of his amours—
he was past middle age. Yet fame coupled with intelligence is an
aphrodisiac for some women.

By all reports Franklin enjoyed flirting with bright and beautiful women. In London—when he was a lobbyist for the colonials—
those amours would have been adulterous because he was still married. Franklin did beg his wife Debbie to sail with him to London,
but his wife was terrified of ship crossings.

Franklin, however, was no "love 'em and leave 'em" Don Juan.
He respected women too much to indulge in one-night stands. The
relationships he enjoyed were intellectual as well as physical. In
London, he romanced Margaret Stevenson, his landlady on Craven
Street.

Some of his other intimate female friends included Countess
Houdtout, an intellect of sixty years who presided over one of
Paris's most famous salons; and Madame Brillon, a quick-witted
beauty who had been traumatized by her husband's attentions to a
mistress. Still another was Madame Helvetius, widow of a French
scientist. These relationships do not prove that he was a womanizer.
In fact, they suggest the opposite. Franklin did not believe in the
one-night stand, and he was no chaser of bimbos, but one who relished the friendship and love of intelligent women.

FINAL FAREWELL

Franklin was one of the most lovable personalities in American
history. He invited not just admiration, but affection. In Philadel-

phia, he became the "City Father" for the innovations he created and the institutions he established there. Philadelphia in his lifetime would become the largest English-speaking city in the world—save London. In Philadelphia Franklin was a frequent sight and tales of his kindnesses abounded among its citizenry.

When Franklin died in 1790, almost twenty thousand of his fellow Philadelphians stopped at his bier to pay their final respects. That was almost one half of the city's entire population!

FOR SHE'S A JOLLY BAD MOTHER . . .

Just before the war, Franklin wrote the following words for his fellow countrymen to sing. They fit the old tune of the English ditty "For He's a Jolly Good Fellow." The first of many verses went:

We have an Old Mother that peevish is grown
She snubs us like Children that scarce walk alone
She forgets we're grown up and have a sense of our own

Which nobody can deny!
Which nobody can deny!

FORK OVER

Franklin was both a consummate diplomat and an inveterate trickster. At a banquet in Paris at the home of a marquis, he put to use both of his arts.

He noticed that a guest had surreptitiously slipped in his pocket a fork of his host's goldware service. Franklin said nothing, but waited for a propitious moment in the dinner conversation. It came when he was asked about his discoveries in electricity.

Franklin, who was considered a wizard because of his many inventions, opined that invention was often a matter of will. For example, he said that by sheer exertion of will, he could effect the displacement of matter.

Franklin took the gold fork at his setting. Holding it in his hand, he asked his listeners to close their eyes and concentrate on the fork. In the meantime he palmed it and let it slide to his sleeve.

Then, with his audience rapt with attention, his eyes turned successively to each diner. When he came to the thieving guest, he intoned, "Let it move to your trousers' pocket."

Franklin then extracted the purloined fork to the wonderment of all.

The thief did not dare reveal his felony. Later Franklin would unobtrusively return his own fork.

FREEDOM FEVER

Among his other talents, Franklin was a songwriter. He even composed some songs in French. While he was in Paris negotiating an end to the Revolutionary War, he discerned the groundswell of sentiment against the aristocratic French monarchy. He sensed the idea of liberty was contagious.

He wrote a ballad whose refrain was "*Ça tiendra*" ("It will catch on").

GINGERBREAD MAN

When Franklin left Boston for Philadelphia as a young man, the ship disembarked at Burlington, New Jersey. This town, on the Delaware River between Philadelphia and Trenton, was a major harbor in colonial days. But it was still twenty miles from

Philadelphia. Franklin lined up in the queue for the ferryboat to Philadelphia, but alas, the boat filled its complement with the passenger just before Franklin. But a woman whose maternal instincts were touched by the forlorn lad gave him her place and a gingerbread cake to sustain him for the trip.

GO FLY A KITE!

Franklin was determined to prove that electricity existed in lightning. Others had tried, including one scientist in Brussels who electrocuted himself in his experiment.

A high place is needed in an electrical storm to attract the lightning. Unfortunately, Quaker Philadelphia was bereft of high steeples. So Franklin came up with the idea of a kite. As the magnet for the lightning he attached a key by string to a kite made of a silk handkerchief supported by two crossed cedar sticks. A wire from the key would extend to a Leyden jar Franklin held in his hand.

On a stormy summer day he dispatched his son William to be ready to run with the kite. Upon the first burst of lightning, he yelled, "Go, Billy, go!" The next flash of lightning ignited sparks on the key and then in the jar. Franklin's published findings on this experiment were the first proof of electricity in lightning.

"GOTTA HAVE HEART!"

Franklin was a Mason, and the central figure in Masonic rites is Solomon, the builder of the temple. Franklin's favorite part of the Bible was Proverbs, which is traditionally considered to be authored by Solomon. Indeed, Proverbs was a source for many of Franklin's adages. Yet some say that Franklin's favorite passage came from the Book of Kings.

In that account, an angel of the Lord appeared to the boy Solomon and asked him, "What gift do you want to rule your country? Riches? Intelligence? Power?" And Solomon replied, "Give me the gift of an understanding heart."

THE GREAT PERSUADER

Some have called President Ronald Reagan the "Great Communicator." Franklin was, however, the "Great Persuader." His powers of suasion broke the deadlocked Philadelphia delegation that swung the biggest colony to the side of independence.

He also convinced France to give the loan that enabled George Washington's Continental Army to stay in the field. Then near the end of his life he helped swing the stalemated Constitutional Convention toward a compromise of two legislative houses.

Thomas Jefferson was once asked the secret of his mentor and his idol's success.

Jefferson said that in his political discussions and debates Franklin never introduced his opinions by saying "Well, it's obvious" or "Anyone should know." Words like "Certainly" or "Undoubtedly" were stricken from his vocabulary.

If someone said something obviously in error such as "Two plus two equals five," the old diplomat might comment, "I can see how one might possibly arrive at that, but . . ." or "I suppose that's one way to look at it, but . . ."

Franklin himself summed it up in his maxim, "Never contradict."

HAIR-RAISING

Franklin as minister to France did not disdain chicanery in his effort to arouse French sentiment in favor of the American colonials. Franklin knew that the British authorities had struck a deal with the Iroquois nation, whose "Long House" Confederation was the dominant Indian power on the Atlantic Coast.

Franklin had been informed that Iroquois chiefs had been selling scalps of slain Americans to British agents.

So Franklin had published an itemized account describing in grisly detail the shipment of mounted tresses of slain American settlers to King George III in England for remittance. The descriptions, from the bills of lading, of young maidens' long gold and chestnut plaits as well as those of hoary old men aroused disgust in France and sentiment for the American cause.

HEARTWARMING

France's lionization of Dr. Franklin began almost as soon as he stepped off the boat at Le Havre. His experiments and writings made the new colonial minister the best-known American, if not the most famous man in the world.

For the radical-chic aristocrats of that day—when the writings of Rousseau were intellectually fashionable—Franklin was a kind of "noble savage" in their idealized conception.

One who initially resisted the adulation of Benjamin Franklin was Count Vergennes, the prime minister whom Franklin had to win over if he was to negotiate a huge loan to finance George Washington's Continental Army in the field.

To win Vergennes, Franklin adopted a ploy he had often used to make friends of foes. Knowing that Vergennes possessed a splendid library, he wrote a letter asking if he might borrow a rare book by a French philosopher. It was subtle praise to the prime minister's ego; Dr. Franklin, the acclaimed American philosopher, had not read the book. And Vergennes was not being asked for a loan of thousands of French francs—just for a book in his library.

Vergennes lent the volume. A couple of weeks later Franklin returned the borrowed book with a letter of appreciation. The ice was broken and the thaw begun. As Franklin observed, "He that has once done you a kindness will be more ready to do you another than he whom you have obliged."

HEIR LOONS?

In the eighteenth century some German universities still held to the quaint practice of allowing the chairs in some academic fields to be passed on to the current chair-holder's eldest son. The mathematics department in one university, for example, had been headed successively by one family for five generations.

When Britain's House of Lords turned deaf ears to the plea of Lord Chatham (William Pitt) to eliminate Parliament's taxation of the colonies, Franklin, outside the legislative chamber, muttered in disgust, "Hereditary legislators."

"Why," said Franklin to a friend, "that's crazier than the hereditary professors of math they have in that college in Germany—because at least they aren't capable of inflicting such harm."

HONOR THY FATHER AND MOTHER
Josiah Franklin
and Abiah, His Wife
Lie here interred
They lived together loving in Wedlock
Fifty-Five Years
Without an Estate or any gainful employment

By constant labour and industry
With God's blessing
They maintained a large family
Comfortably
And brought up thirteen children
and seven Grandchildren
Reputably
From this Instance, Reader
Be encouraged to Diligence in thy Calling
And Distrust not Providence
He was a pious and prudent man
She a discreet and virtuous woman
Their youngest son
In filial regard to their Memory
Places this Stone
J.F. born 1655 Died 1744 Aetat 89
A.F. born 1667 Died 1752 Aetat 85

HOW NOW, BROWN COWS?

King George III and his new tax policy on the American colonists prompted Franklin to spin a fable about how a farmer treated his cows. Though the owner was prospering with the herd's milk production, he thought he could squeeze even more from his land by taking the grass the cows grazed upon and selling it for hay. The result was that what little milk the cows then could produce they used to suckle themselves.

For Franklin, the moral of the story was that the oppressive tax policies of "Farmer George" (George III's nickname in the colonies) would force his herd in America to go it alone.

"HOW TO WIN FOES AND OFFEND PEOPLE"

In a reverse of Dale Carnegie, Franklin once wrote a tract called "Rules for Making Oneself a Disagreeable Companion." Some of the pointers included:

1. If possible engross the whole discourse . . . talk of much of yourself, your education, your knowledge, your successes . . .
2. When you are out of breath, watch his words, and you will probably find something to contradict and raise a dispute on. If that fails, criticize his grammar.
3. If another shall be saying an indisputably good thing—say it has already been said by Bacon, Locke, or another eminent writer—and thus you deprive him of the reputation he might have gained from it.

HUMBLE PIE

The religion of Franklin was good character and good works. After much deliberation he set down twelve principles that he entitled "The Art of Virtue":

1. Temperance	5. Frugality	9. Moderation
2. Silence	6. Industry	10. Cleanliness
3. Order	7. Sincerity	11. Tranquillity
4. Resolution	8. Justice	12. Chastity

He then showed the list to a Quaker friend, who shook his head and said, "Benjamin, thee has forgotten humility."

So the chastened Franklin added a thirteenth, "Humility."

"I" OR "U"

Does the Declaration of Independence read that people are endowed by certain "inalienable rights" or "unalienable" rights? Well, Jefferson wrote "inalienable" and so it is carved on the

Jefferson Memorial in Washington. But the original signed copy residing in the National Archives says "unalienable."

Franklin, who was the chief editor on the small committee that reviewed the young Jefferson's draft, revised it.

Why did he substitute "unalienable" for "inalienable"? Although there is no direct evidence of Franklin's thought on that matter, it may have been another example of Franklin's wisdom. "Inalienable" is a legal word in use today that defines rights of property that cannot be involuntarily taken away. One can, however, assign such an "inalienable" deed in a conveyance or will or give that right away.

"Unalienable," on the other hand, is an archaic eighteenth-century word that defines rights given by God that cannot be yielded but must be preserved for posterity. This thinking foreshadows Franklin's warning to the assembled throng outside the State House in 1787: "A republic—if you can keep it!"

Franklin refined some other Jefferson phrases. For example, he altered "sacred and undeniable" to "self-evident."

JOHN-NIE ON THE SPOT

King Louis XVI noted the absence and disaffection of a paramour. He was informed that a *petite amie* of his was enamored of Dr. Franklin.

On her forthcoming birthday the king sent her a gift—a Sèvres porcelain chamberpot with a likeness of Franklin at the bottom.

LATIN LOVER?

The practical Franklin saw no purpose in studying a dead language such as Latin. He did speak French, read Spanish, and have a smattering of Italian, but disdained the learning of Latin.

Yet when he chose the motto of the new United States, he wrote it in Latin, *"E pluribus unum."*

LOVE AT FIRST HATE

When a hungry Ben Franklin first arrived in Philadelphia, the first thing he did was buy four loaves of bread with his remaining pennies to last him for the day. The bread in Philadelphia, unlike the round pie-shaped loaves in Boston, resembled a blunderbuss musket—almost as long as one's arm.

Gobbling up one loaf, he stuck two others under his arms, with a third held under his chin. The scruffy-looking seventeen-year-old was a comic sight.

The extra shirt he needed for his new home he had stuffed under the shirt he was wearing, and the spare socks and underclothes he squeezed into his sleeves. The disheveled appearance was not enhanced by a dirty face, which had not seen soap and water in his days on ship.

As he walked up Philadelphia's High (now Market) Street with the long loaves between arms and under chin, he sighted a pretty girl and gave her a wink. The young woman responded by pointing her nose to the sky in utter scorn.

Franklin chuckled and walked on. The first quest for the apprentice printer was to find lodging. After inquiries, he was told to look up Mr. Read, who had a spare room to rent out.

The next morning when he came down the stairs in his new lodgings with Mr. Read to eat his breakfast, he found to his surprise that his breakfast mate was the young woman who had spurned his once-over glance the day before. Yet the hate at first sight soon turned to love, for Debbie Read would later become Franklin's wife.

NO SMALL POTATOES

It is amazing to think that potatoes, which are now a staple, were avoided like poison in the eighteenth century. The farmers believed an old wives' tale that potatoes caused leprosy.

A promoter of the potato was a French farmer by the name of Parmentier. He believed that the tuber could be the salvation of French agriculture, but his efforts to persuade farmers had met a cool response.

Franklin, an amateur agriculturist, came to the rescue. He suggested that Parmentier cook up a banquet with every course made of potatoes. Franklin, who was then the pet of Paris, would attend as the honored guest. Franklin came and gave every entrée a rave review.

Franklin especially touted the bread, which was made out of ground flour from potatoes. The popular American guest also toasted the dinner with a fermented potato potable (not unlike vodka).

News of the event swept France and soon farmers were stealing potatoes grown in Parmentier's experimental fields. Potatoes soon became a Parisian passion.

OPEN OR SHUT?

In all his political career Franklin suffered only one defeat. In 1764 he was narrowly defeated for reelection to his General Assembly seat. For some years he had been the champion of the anti-Proprietary party that insisted that the lands owned by the Penn family and the rest of the original Proprietors be subject to taxes like those of other landowners. In this cause he had been joined by the Scotch-Irish as well as the Amish and Mennonite settlers from Germany.

But the aristocratic faction mounted a vicious campaign to unseat the popular Franklin. They spread tales among the Quakers of Franklin's debaucheries. The principal canard was that Franklin had abandoned a young servant he got pregnant and later had buried her in an unmarked grave.

For the Scotch-Irish the Proprietors reprinted and circulated Franklin's earlier editorials denouncing their massacres of Indian tribes in central Pennsylvania. Then for the Germans they republished a Pennsylvania *Gazette* editorial by Franklin warning that the prolific farmer immigration from the Palatinate area might eventually make Pennsylvania a predominantly German-speaking colony.

Despite the Proprietors' efforts, the popular affection for Franklin would have still insured his victory but for a mistake by his campaign managers. At two in the morning the aristocratic party asked that the polling stations be shut. Franklin's managers, noting that there were some old and feeble citizens who had been waiting for hours in the long polling lines, opted to keep the polling booths open. As a result, his Proprietary opponents sent horses to Germantown—a section of Philadelphia—to bring out some anti-Franklin voters among the German-speaking population. Their votes in the wee hours of the morning were the decisive edge in Franklin's twenty-six-vote defeat.

A PAINE IN THE A__?

On his many visits to England, Franklin became familiar with one of the British Custom House agents. The young official expressed boredom with his duties, and Franklin encouraged him to take up the trade of printing and come to America.

The agent did, and his publication condemning the "sunshine patriots" in the dark days of Valley Forge was one of the most successful propaganda pamphlets of the Revolutionary War.

Yet as Franklin admired Thomas Paine for his revolutionary goals, he also thought he was a gadfly—often counterproductive in his efforts.

Paine would not mute his atheism or later his support for Revolutionary France. His subjects for attack would include not only George Washington, but even his old sponsor Franklin.

PET CEMETERY

Children loved Franklin and he reciprocated that affection with a childlike passion for both pets and rhyming poesy. He once kept a mouse as a little friend. To the children of his friends in London, he sent as a gift an American squirrel he called "Skug," the Indian name for the gray squirrel.

A year later he received from the English children a report of Skug's unhappy demise. He wrote the children his condolences and suggested a burial with this epitaph:

Here lies Skug
As Snug
As a Bug
In a Rug.

"A 'PIECE' THAT PASSETH ALL UNDERSTANDING . . ."

William Temple Franklin, called Temple, was the love child of William Franklin, who in turn had been illegitimately sired by Benjamin Franklin.

As envoy to Paris, Ben Franklin's relations with son Billy were strained when William, as royal governor of New Jersey, sided with Britain. As war broke out, William Franklin was forced to move to London. There his son Temple was born.

Franklin embraced his grandson and had him brought to France to live with him. The boy learned to speak French as a native.

On one occasion Ben Franklin was invited to hear some prize-day recitals at a French finishing school for young French ladies. Each recited a piece from French poets or playwrights. There was one selection at which Franklin clapped most heartily.

Temple tugged his grandfather's sleeve and asked him why. Franklin, whose hearing as well as comprehension of spoken French was less than his grandson's, in embarrassment whispered, "It was the only one I didn't understand so I compensated by applauding the longest."

"But Grandpapa," Temple replied, "she was reciting an essay from one of your own writings."

PIPE DREAM

As a young boy Ben saved his pennies doing odd jobs in addition to working for his father. One day he saw and heard a sailor, just off a ship, playing a hornpipe. Ben had to have it! He ran home to retrieve his hoard of coins and spent all of it for this instrument.

Not only did the family soon tire of the shrill tones, but so did

Ben. It was a lesson Ben would remember the rest of his life: not to blow hard-earned savings on an impulse for ephemeral pleasure.

PLAYING POSSUM

By the middle of the 1780s the new government of the United States was foundering. The Continental Congress lacked the central authority to bind the new thirteen states.

In 1785 at Annapolis, Maryland, two young lawyers—Alexander Hamilton from New York and James Madison from Virginia—met to discuss ways to strengthen the Articles of Confederation, the young nation's ten-year-old charter. Their conclusion: Draft a new constitution.

Franklin let his name be put forth as a candidate to be a delegate to the convention, but he did not campaign. He let word spread that his age had enfeebled him to the point where he was just about completely bedridden. The story was not quite the truth.

Actually the astute Franklin used his infirmity to dodge questioning of his views. Conservatives would deem his championship for a wider voting franchise distasteful, and liberals would find his conversion to a need for a central executive a betrayal. To liberals any executive spelled K-I-N-G. Partly because Franklin managed to avoid giving away his positions, his election was a romp. No one liked to vote against the grand old man, and anyway they convinced themselves that the stricken Franklin would probably not even make it to the State House proceedings. Franklin deserved election if only for symbolic reasons.

Franklin fooled them. Following his election, he ordered a sedan chair to be shipped from France that could carry him to the convention sessions, since he could not walk or ride a horse. Then he retained the lawyer James Wilson—who had also been elected a delegate—to act as his advocate and legal draftsman to effect the changes Franklin wanted. No delegate was more satisfied with the way the document turned out than the convention's oldest delegate.

POOR RICHARD AND RICH BEN

Was Poor Richard an alter ego for Benjamin Franklin? Franklin was no more Richard Saunders than Arthur Conan Doyle was Sherlock Holmes or Ian Fleming was James Bond. Such fictional characters might have made their creators rich, but they were purely products of imagination, not self-portraits. Conan Doyle was a country doctor, not a London sleuth; Ian Fleming a paunchy novelist, not a dashing spy; and Franklin was a successful printer and publisher, not a henpecked Quaker astronomer.

As in the case of Sherlock Holmes, the readers of Franklin's almanac believed in the existence of Richard Saunders and his scolding wife, Bridget, and Franklin fed the myth.

Franklin was not a Quaker. Nor was he tyrannized by a termagant wife. And he was not poor—a subject for sympathy—either in his marital or financial status.

Poor Richard was a personality whose biographical details farmers knew more about than those of George Washington or King George III. Yet essentially he was a ploy Franklin created to add spice to the almanac and widen readership.

RING OF TRUTH

In 1749, a legislative matter came up for vote in the Pennsylvania State House in Philadelphia—not a tariff or a tax, but a routine bill to purchase a bell.

One legislator who voted for the bell was Franklin. Although in his first term, Franklin had for over a decade served as the clerk of the house—a strategic post for one who was a printer by profession.

The bell was brought from England and a biblical inscription for the lip of the bell was picked from Leviticus: "Proclaim liberty to all the lands and all the inhabitants thereof."

Franklin would make that bell inscription ring prophetically true—not just once but twice: first when he broke the tie in the Pennsylvania delegation to put the largest colony on the side of independence, and again when he supported the two-house compromise that ended the deadlock in the Constitutional Convention.

"ROCK AROUND THE CLOCK"

A Massachusetts clergyman named Cutler came to Philadelphia to meet the colonies' most famous citizen. Since Cutler was an amateur scientist, he was anxious to see some of Franklin's discoveries and inventions.

Franklin first showed him a two-headed snake he had embalmed in alcohol and then took him to look over his library of over four thousand books. Cutler was also fascinated by Franklin's "artificial arm" that he had invented for taking down books from high shelves.

In addition, Cutler was impressed with the glass machine Franklin exhibited for showing the circulation of blood in the veins and arteries. Cutler also enjoyed seeing the rolling press Franklin had devised for copying of letters.

When Cutler returned home, he was asked by Bostonians what was Franklin's most impressive invention. He replied, "The rocker." The rocking chair was a great armed chair with rockers and a large fan attached to the top of it that was controlled by foot pedals.

"The chair," Cutler enthused later to his listeners, "it even has a fan that keeps you cool and the bugs away!"

SABBATH AND SATAN

On January 17, 1706, Abiah Folger Franklin gave birth to her seventh son. Yet her husband, Josiah, did not boast of the good news to friends and neighbors. What should have been a day of delight was a time for despair. The boy was born on a Sunday. Even for the pious Puritans, religion was often streaked with superstition. It was widely believed that a child born on a Sunday was conceived on a Sunday. Such a sin on the Sabbath was more than wrong, it was wicked. A boy born on a Sunday was a son of Satan—to be shunned, scorned, and watched with suspicion.

Despite the wintry chill of that January day, Josiah Franklin wrapped up the newly born child in the warmest blankets he could find and then brooked the frigid winds to have him baptized in the church. Since most christenings occurred at least three days following the birth, no one in the congregation had an inkling that the baby christened as Benjamin had been born only hours before.

SECRET SWINGER?

Did Benjamin Franklin cavort with the revelers of the Hell-Fire Club? The English society, which was limited to twelve members, shrouded their blasphemous activities in secrecy. Their skits and ceremonies mocked religion and the clergy.

Their headquarters—which made their doings more impious—was an old abbey near High Wycombe in Buckinghamshire built by the Cistercian monks in 1145. The high priest or monk superior was Sir Francis Dashwood, later Lord Le Despenser. The fact that he was the frequent weekend host of Franklin lends credence to the idea that Franklin might have attended some of the society's rites.

Another member was John Wilkes, for whom Wilkes-Barre was named. He was an ardent advocate of the colonial cause. Though Franklin was wary of the demagogic Wilkes, he did work with him on legislative maneuvers. A rake as well as a radical, Wilkes would brag that he was the most accomplished seducer in London. In the annals of the Hell-Fire Club, Wilkes was remembered for escorting a baboon dressed in a devil's costume.

Despite the moralizing through the mouth of Poor Richard, Franklin was no prig. Though a lusty man, he was assiduously discreet in his affairs. Self-discipline was his essential code. Still, the meetings of the Hell-Fire Club offered great opportunities for private lobbying away from the House of Commons. Since the Hell-Fire members rejected authority, including the king and the church, they might well be sympathetic to the Americans. If they were libertines, they were also lovers of liberty.

There is no absolute proof that Franklin visited the nefarious abbey. Yet since he was often a houseguest of Sir Francis Dashwood, it is likely that he was an occasional observer if not a participant in activities that were blasphemous as well as bawdy.

SNAKE IN THE GRASS

Franklin was angered by the British practice of sending convicts to America. Traveling to Georgia in his duties as postmaster general, he saw firsthand the English establishment of a penal colony.

The British authorities finally ended the wretched practice in 1750. Perhaps they were influenced by a threat by Franklin to send over one rattlesnake to be dropped in Hyde Park as a payoff for every convict shipped to America.

SOAP OPERA

A soap maker came to Franklin with a problem. Though he had advertised its special cleansing properties, it had failed to catch on in the Pennsylvania market.

It is the women who buy soap, Franklin explained to the businessman, and it is the women whose fancy you must arouse.

All soap products claim to clean, but you should assert that your soap is the only one that will leave their feminine hands not raw and chapped but softer and smoother. Appeal, said Franklin, to the romance in women.

Franklin rewrote the soap advertisements and the soap merchant "cleaned up" with his expanded sales.

"STAGGERED AND STEWED"

Franklin first got drunk when he was seventeen, on rum—the poison of choice in colonial days. For the rest of his life his habits were generally abstemious—except for an occasional glass of Madeira. Still, from that drunken orgy in his youth, Franklin began to compile synonyms for the word *drunk*. Some of these follow:

Addled
Almost froze
Among the Philistines

Boozy
Cherry-merry
Chipper
Cogey
Confoundedly cut
Disguised
Feverish
Foxed
Fuddled
Glazed
Groatable
Half-seas over
In the suds
In their altitudes
Jambled
Juicy
Loose in the hilts
Lordly
Lost his rudder
Maudlin
Mellow
Nim-topsical
Oiled
Pretty well-entered
Raddled
See the sun
See two moons
Skin-ful
Stewed

Swampt
The sun has shone on them
Tipsy
Wet

STERLING CONTRIBUTION

Franklin was a practical man who had little use for the pedagogues—particularly academics who required that Latin be the
central core of any curriculum. Yet the name of Franklin will
always be associated with Boston Latin, the oldest school in
Massachusetts.

In his will he bequeathed money to that school of his native city
providing that silver medals be awarded to the outstanding students of the senior class. The Franklin medal is still the highest
recognition given at Boston Latin today.

"SWEET LAND OF LIBERTY"

Public Enemy Number One, in the eyes of two successive
French kings, was Voltaire, the atheist free thinker and philosopher.
Voltaire was imprisoned in the Bastille in his twenties, and after-
ward spent much of his life in Switzerland. As a dying man,
Voltaire was allowed back to his native land.

Franklin, who admired the writings of Voltaire, was warned that
any attempt by the American envoy to see Voltaire would be
viewed as an affront to King Louis XVI, who had recently given his
assent to recognition of the American nation.

Despite the risk, Franklin called on the dying Voltaire. Franklin
took with him his grandson, Temple Franklin (the illegitimate
child of his illegitimate son William).

On his deathbed, Voltaire, a supporter of the American cause, summoned up the language he hadn't used in years to give his benediction to the boy in English:

"To God and Liberty."

TALL TAIL

In the art of public relations, Franklin had a variety of tricks in his repertoire: satire, spoof, fable, and sometimes a hoax.

While in London, Colonial Agent Franklin wanted to convince Britain that the American colonies were too rich in assets to drive into independence.

One item he had printed in the London papers was about the incredible breed of indigenous sheep in America. "The tail," said the article of this native sheep, "grew so fat with wool that a cart had to be attached to carry the tail."

THANKSGIVING DAY PRAYER

At age twenty-two, Franklin composed a prayer to be used at the end of harvest:

For peace and liberty, for food and
raiment, for corn and wine and milk
and every other nourishment
Good God I thank Thee

For the common benefits of air and
light, for useful fire and delicious water
Good God I thank Thee

For knowledge and literature and
every useful art, for my friends, and their
prosperity and for the fewness of my enemies
Good God I thank Thee

For all the innumerable benefits,
for life, for reason, for health,
for joy and every pleasant hour
Good God I thank Thee

THE TURKEY'S NOT A "TURKEY"

Despite Franklin's efforts, the nation chartered under the new Constitution chose the bald eagle as its symbol on coins and dollars. Franklin was dismayed; he had lobbied hard for his choice—the turkey.

To Franklin, the eagle was a cousin of the vulture, a "bad" bird whose way of life was stealing, plundering, and killing.

"The humble turkey," said Franklin, "minds his own business, respecting the rights of others." Furthermore, argued Franklin, "the turkey is a unique American creature."

VALET OF VALUE

While Minister to France, Franklin was warned that his valet was a spy on the payroll of the British. Repeatedly Franklin was urged to dismiss the servant. Franklin demurred.

He answered, "You know he is a spy. I know he is a spy. But he doesn't know that we know it. There are some things I want the British to know—that they would dismiss if we said them but accept if they bought them from a spy. And not only that," Franklin said with a laugh, "but he's a good valet."

WHO WAS BILLY'S MOTHER?

There has always been some mystery as to the identity of William Franklin's mother. The foes of Benjamin Franklin circulated the story that she was a servant girl in the house Franklin moved into when he returned from London in 1729. In the only election Franklin ever lost—his reelection bid for Pennsylvania General Assembly in 1764—political enemies rumored that he neglected the wretched mother of his child and let her die in penury and then buried her in an unmarked grave.

Yet the available facts tend to disprove the household girl canard. William Franklin was born about the time Ben took Deborah Read as his common-law wife. In a letter William Franklin wrote in 1812, he stated, "I am in my 82nd year." So Billy had been born about 1730.

Deborah, moreover, recognized him as her son. Referring to Billy, she wrote in 1751 to William Strahan, the publisher and friend of her husband, "My son has gone to Boston to visit friends." Deborah Franklin died on December 14, 1774, and William Franklin wrote his father in London, "I came here [Philadelphia] Thursday to attend the funeral of my poor old mother." Arguably one can suggest that both William and Deborah abhorred the cold terms *stepmother* and *stepson*. On the other hand, the pregnancy of Deborah with William might have impelled Franklin to take Deborah as his wife.

WITHOUT LICENSE

An old schoolboy chant used to run:

Benjamin Franklin was born in Boston.
He moved to Philadelphia.
He married.
Then *he discovered electricity.*

Of course, he didn't discover electricity—he only discovered electricity in lightning.

Furthermore, he had no marriage ceremony. At age twenty-one, when Franklin sailed from Philadelphia to London in a quest for better printing presses, he left a tearful Debbie in his wake.

Deborah Read was the pretty lass he sighted just after he stepped off the boat in Philadelphia and who, by strange coincidence, would turn out to be the daughter of his landlord.

Debbie thought she had an understanding with Ben, but as the months of Franklin's sojourn in London extended into years without a letter, she despaired and married a man named Rogers who was a potter by trade. But the potter was a rotter! He went off to sea, abandoning her. When Franklin returned from London, he found his old girlfriend in tears—deserted and distressed.

Yet the practical Ben would find a solution. Their marital relationship would be common-law—without license, church, and wedding. Any other marriage rite might have been null; it took seven years for desertion to end a marriage. But if Benjamin and Deborah lived together, presenting themselves to the public as man and wife, the relationship would ripen legally into a common-law marriage. So Ben and Debbie became partners—setting up shop and house together. And not altogether incidentally, Deborah would give a home to Billy, Franklin's illegitimate son who may or may not have been her child.

Patriots and Tories

Perhaps no one in the eighteenth century met and knew more of the famous than Benjamin Franklin. Because of his span of life, his breadth of interests, and his frequent travels, Franklin had an unmatched range of acquaintances.

From Cotton Mather, whose sermons thundered from his New England pulpit in the late seventeenth century, to James Madison, the fourth U.S. president in the nineteenth century, Franklin had acquaintanceship with many leaders who, like himself, shaped our history.

Governor Thomas Penn, the son of Pennsylvania founder William, called Franklin an enemy, and just before he died at his seat in the House chamber in 1848, John Quincy Adams, the sixth president, talked of the conversations he had had with Franklin while clerking for his father in Paris.

As the world's most famous citizen, Franklin was feted by kings of Europe, consulted by its philosophers, and read by its scientists.

David Hume, the Scottish philosopher and historian, counted Franklin as a friend. Voltaire hailed him as a champion of liberty. Joseph Priestly, the discoverer of oxygen, entertained him at his

English home, as did Josiah Wedgwood, who pioneered a new way of making china.

Franklin knew personalities of the day ranging from Boswell, Samuel Johnson's friend and biographer, to Baron Munchausen, the fabled German mythomaniac.

Yet for one who knew Founding Fathers such as George Wash-ing-ton, John Adams, Thomas Jefferson, and Alexander Hamilton in this country; William Pitt, George Grenville, and John Wilkes in Britain; and King Louis XVI, Voltaire, and Lafayette in France, Franklin's observations on the leading figures of the time are sparse and guarded.

The uneducated son of a Boston candlemaker found himself late in life received by the court of Versailles and honored by the elite and eminent of Paris. Yet Franklin didn't make that ascent from crafts-man to statesman by loosening his lips or stepping on others' toes.

A master of public relations, Franklin was brilliant in promoting himself—but never at the expense of others. A born diplomat, he listened while others gossiped. He asked questions and let others do the talking.

He refrained from making public speeches, and what talking he did was in private. He preferred the written page, where he had the time to deliberate before he put his comments to paper. Even then, most of his quotations are written under the guise of another per-sonality, Poor Richard. Even aside from his almanac, Franklin was one of the most voluminous writers of his day. His comments on contemporaries, however, are few and limited. Only by diligent research are his views on public figures unearthed. Even then they do not always carry the snap and wit that would be expected of America's first humorist.

Like Winston Churchill in the twentieth century, Franklin was a Renaissance man and world leader whose span of services in the public arena were unparalleled in his day. But Franklin was no aristocrat. He was a self-made man with no connections by birth or family. Unlike the outspoken Churchill, Franklin always followed the advice that Cotton Mather gave him as a young man: "Duck." Franklin did not make his way to the top by inviting trouble or asking for enemies. As a result, his comments about others were muted.

≈≈ ≈≈ ≈≈

JOHN ADAMS (1735–1826) *Fellow peace commissioner with Franklin and second president of the United States*

☞ Always an honest man, often a great man, but sometimes out of his senses.

WILLIAM ALLEN (1704–1780) *One of the Pennsylvania Proprietors, Pennsylvania jurist, and builder of the State House (Independence Hall)*

☞ He has the wisest look of any man I know and if he would only nod and wink and could but hold his tongue, he might deceive an angel.

BENEDICT ARNOLD (1741–1801) *American revolutionary general and traitor*

☞ He lives covered with his infamy and despised even by those who expected to be served by his treachery.

GENERAL EDWARD BRADDOCK (1695–1755) *British general in the French and Indian War*

☞ The general was, I think, a brave man and might probably have made a figure as a good officer in some European war. But he had too much self-confidence, too high an opinion of the validity of regular troops, and too mean [low] an opinion of both Americans and Indians.

LORD CAMDEN (Charles Pratt; 1714–1794) *First Earl of Camden, chief judge, and pro-American British leader in the House of Lords*

☞ A wonderfully good speaker and able reasoner.

SIR FRANCIS DASHWOOD (Lord Le Despenser; 1710–1777) *A member of the Hell-Fire Club and occasional weekend host of Franklin*

☞ The kind countenance, the facetious, and very intelligent conversation of mine host who having been many years engaged on public affairs, seen in all parts of Europe, and kept the best company in the world and is himself the best existing.

SILAS DEANE (1737–1789) *U.S. peace commissioner and American diplomat*

☞ I esteem him a faithful, active, and able minister.

☞ To me it appears your resentments and passions have overcome your reason and judgment.

ABIAH FOLGER FRANKLIN (1667–1752) *Franklin's mother*

☞ She was a discreet and virtuous woman.

JOSIAH FRANKLIN (1657–1745) *Franklin's father*

☞ He was a pious and prudent man.

GEORGE III (1738–1820) *King of England, 1760–1820*

☞ The very best in the world and the most amiable. [Written at the time of his accession.]

☞ Hatred of this country is the constant object of his mind.

☞ That a single man in England should have been permitted to destroy near one hundred thousand human creatures!

GEORGE GRENVILLE (1753–1813) *Marquess of Buckingham, British peace commissioner, and later prime minister*

☞ Mr. Grenville appeared to me a sensible, judicious, intelligent, good tempered, and well instructed young man.

LORD HILLSBOROUGH (1701–1776) *British Secretary of State for America*

☞ I know him to be as two-faced and deceitful as any man I ever knew. His character is conceit, wrong-headedness, obstinacy, and passion.

DAVID HUME (1711–1776) *Scottish philosopher and historian*

☞ But that excellent Christian,[1] David Hume, agreeable to the

---

[1] David Hume was called mockingly by Scottish Presbyterians "St. David." Hume, whose objectivist philosophy was skeptical of biblical miracles and other phenomena such as the virgin birth, was denounced for his atheist views. An Anglican, he was no more an atheist than Franklin. Franklin, in calling Hume an "excellent Christian," is replying to Hume's critics. The street on which Hume lived is still named St. David's Street, which it was called sarcastically in the philosopher's day.

precepts of the Gospel, has received the stranger and I now live with him at his house in the Newtown [section of Edinburgh] most happily.

JOHN PAUL JONES (1747–1792) *American captain and naval hero*

꘠ If you should observe on occasion to give your officers and friends a little more praise than is their due, and confess more faults that you can be justly charged with, you will become a great captain.

SIR WILLIAM KEITH (1680–1749) *Governor of Pennsylvania*

꘠ Sir William wished to please everybody, and having little to give, he gave instead expectations.

LAFAYETTE, THE MARQUIS OF (1757–1834) *French general in the American Revolution*

꘠ I admire much the activity of your genius and the strong desire you have of being continually employed against our common enemy.

꘠ He is exceedingly beloved and everybody's good wishes attend him. . . . He has left a beautiful wife, and for her sake particularly, we hope that his bravery and his ardent desire to distinguish himself will be a little restrained by the General's prudence.

ARTHUR LEE (1740–1792) *U.S. peace commissioner in France*[2]

꘠ In sowing suspicions and jealousies, in creating misunder-

---

[2] Lee was jealous of Franklin and he ever sought to diminish Franklin's influence

standings and quarrels, in malice and subtlety and indefatigable industry, he has no equal.

LOUIS XV (1710–1774) *King of France, 1715–1774*

☞ Louis the 15th, present King of France, called His Most Christian Majesty, he bids fair to be as great a mischief maker as his great-grandfather [Louis XIV].

REVEREND COTTON MATHER (1663–1728) *Puritan theologian and preacher*

☞ He was a man that never missed any occasion of giving instruction.

THOMAS PAINE (1737–1809) *Revolutionary propagandist*

☞ He that spits in the wind, spits in his own face.

THOMAS PENN (1702–1775) *Proprietor, governor of Pennsylvania, son of William Penn*

☞ I was astonished to see him meanly give up his father's character and conceived for him a more cordial and thorough contempt for him than I have ever felt for anyone else.

Thomas was a miserable churl—always intent on grasping and saving—whatever good the father may have done for the province was amply undone by the mischief of the son.

---

by planting rumors about him with British counterparts in negotiating the end of the Revolutionary War.

WILLIAM PITT (Lord Chatham; 1708–1778) *British prime minister and friend of America*

∛ He was then too great a man or too much occupied in affairs of great moment.[3]

∛ He impressed me with the highest idea of him as a great and most able statesman.

DR. JOSEPH PRIESTLY (1733–1804) *Scientist and discoverer of oxygen*

∛ I should rejoice much, if I could once more recover the leisure to search with you into the works of nature.

∛ I always rejoice to hear of your still being employed in experimental researches into nature and the success you meet with.

LORD SHIRLEY, WILLIAM (1694–1771) *Colonial governor of Massachusetts and commander-in-chief of North America in the French and Indian War*

∛ I take him to be a wise and good and worthy man. He is being made the subject of some public, virulent, and senseless libel.

REVEREND WILLIAM SMITH (1727–1803) *President, College of Philadelphia; later president of Washington College in Chestertown, Maryland*

∛ I made that man my enemy by doing him too much kindness.[4]

---

[3] Franklin, in his first years as colonial agent for Pennsylvania, could not engage Pitt's interest in American problems.

[4] Franklin was responsible for Smith being appointed head of the College of Philadelphia (later the University of Pennsylvania). Yet Smith intrigued against Franklin, spreading slanderous rumors.

MARGARET STEVENSON (1718–1777) *Franklin's London landlady*

∛ She is very obliging, takes great care of my health, and is very diligent when I am in any way indisposed, but yet I have a thousand times wished I had you with me.[5]

COMTE DE VERGENNES (1717–1787) *French prime minister*

∛ So wise and so good a man taken away from the station he filled is a great loss not only to France but to Europe in general, to America and to mankind.

SIR ROBERT WALPOLE (1676–1745) *British prime minister*

∛ Walpole had humanity enough to reject the proposal often made to him by his hungry hangers-on of taxing the colonies.

GEORGE WASHINGTON (1732–1799) *General and first president of the United States*

∛ General Washington is the man that our eyes are fixed on for President and what little influence I have is devoted to him.

∛ My fine crab-tree walking-stick with a gold head curiously wrought in the form of the cap of liberty I give to my friend and the friend of mankind, George Washington. . . . If it were a scepter, he has merited it and would become it.[6]

---

[5] Franklin was trying to assure his wife Deborah that his relationship with Peggy Stevenson was platonic.

[6] Franklin's will bequeathed General Washington his cane.

◌ You would, at this side of the sea, enjoy the reputation you have acquired, pure and free from those little shades that the jealousy and envy of a man's countrymen and contemporaries are ever endeavoring to cast over living merit. Here you will know, and enjoy what posterity will say of Washington. For a thousand leagues have nearly the same effect as a thousand years.

REVEREND GEORGE WHITFIELD (1714–1770) *Preacher and evangelist*
◌ His eloquence had a wonderful power over the hearts and purses of his hearers.

JOHN WILKES (1725–1797) *British radical parliamentarian*
◌ His mobs are patrolling the streets—some knocking all down that will not roar for Wilkes; courts of justice afraid to give judgment against him.

Renaissance Roles

Though he authored the sayings of Poor Richard, Franklin in his own life did not always practice what Poor Richard preached. Yet if he was not a paragon, he was a polygon. He was a multifaceted genius who is often described as a Renaissance man.

The prototype originated in the early sixteenth century with Michelangelo and Leonardo da Vinci. Late in that century, as the Renaissance spread from Florentine Italy to Elizabethan London, the type expanded to include men like Francis Bacon and Sir Walter Raleigh. Bacon was a politician, philosopher, and scientist. Raleigh, among other talents, was both poet and pirate.

In our own history we associate the term "Renaissance man" with the eighteenth century—the time of our Founding Fathers. Two of them—Benjamin Franklin and his protégé Thomas Jefferson—stand preeminent.

Today in the technological twentieth century, the Renaissance man—with the singular exception of Winston Churchill—seems nonexistent. Although this author is hardly a genius and makes no claim to an unmediocre range of talent, I have been a lawyer, actor, legislator, diplomat, professor, author, and even an illustrator, and I know from firsthand experience that this age of specialization looks askance at any contributions outside one's chosen niche of expertise and professional training.

Fortunately, the eighteenth century entertained no such prejudice. Franklin, who had the sparsest of schooling, was welcomed into the British Royal Society, Europe's most elite society of scientists and academicians.

Franklin, through his writings, was the most famous colonial American. In his adopted city of Philadelphia, he was esteemed for the variety of civic improvements he championed. So it was only natural that Philadelphia—the largest city and virtual capital of the colonies—would turn to Franklin for any tough or delicate assignment.

Whether it was settling Indian disputes, establishing a postal system, arranging a deal for General Braddock with the German settlers, or persuading France to come in on the side of the new United States, Franklin was the man they turned to. He was America's first troubleshooter.

Certainly Franklin was a jack of all trades—printer, craftsman, merchant, journalist—but he was also "Ben of all talents," who possessed the genius of an inventor, the brilliance of a scientist, and the persuasive flair of a born diplomat. In a young country there was a vacuum of leadership. Hospitals had to be built, colleges established, state charters as well as national constitutions drafted, and treaties negotiated.

It has been written that the collection of political minds that met to write the Constitution were at least the equal to anything the British or the French could offer at the time. Yet Franklin was recognized as the giant of both the Continental Congress in 1776 that drafted the Declaration of Independence and the convention eleven years later that framed the Constitution. Franklin was the only signer of all five documents that created America: the Declaration of Independence, the Articles of Confederation, the treaty with France that recognized the United States as a sovereign nation, the treaty to conclude the war with England, and the Constitution.

Statesmanship was just one of the gifts possessed by this Renaissance man. Yet his selection for such a political role came to him in part due to his prowess in other efforts. It was his devices as an inventor, his improvements as a civic leader, his findings as a scientist, and his popularity as a writer that led his contemporaries to believe that Franklin could come up with a solution to just about every problem. And Franklin gloried in each challenge. Optimistic by instinct, fearless by nature, and self-confident in any undertaking, Franklin eliminated the thought of failure from his philosophy. A can-do type, Franklin tried doing just about everything and, more often than not, succeeded.

਼ ਼ ਼

ADVERTISING EXECUTIVE

Franklin could write the punchy one-liner that is the hallmark of a good copywriter today. He devised ads in his newspaper promoting his almanac. He also rewrote the merchants' offers into catchy advertisements.

It was also Franklin who first introduced contests to increase circulation rewards and to give away subscriptions as prizes.

AGRICULTURIST

Franklin was a great advocate of maize—the native American grain we call corn and think of as a vegetable. He publicized the many uses of corn: hominy, cornbread, corn pudding, succotash, hoe cake, meal mush, corn syrup, roast corn, boiled corn, as well as corn on the cob.

He introduced into this country such European vegetables as Scottish cabbage, kohlrabi, and Chinese rhubarb. He was also the American pioneer of artificial fertilizer, which he used on his New Jersey farm near Burlington.

AUTHOR

In his day Franklin was the best-selling author. He wrote the first publication to reach all thirteen colonies. Also, his *Autobiography* not only was the top seller of his day in America, but also in Europe, where it was translated into French, Spanish, and German. In addition, Franklin penned a series of political satires that rank with such contemporaries as Jonathan Swift and Lord Chesterfield.

BUSINESSMAN

A century and a half before Horatio Alger ever appeared in print, Franklin was the first rags-to-riches American success story. A printer by trade, he became shopkeeper, merchant, manufacturer, and publisher. His formula of keeping long hours, low expenses, and a high rate of savings has never been improved on. His print shop expanded into the selling of ink, pens, candles, and books. He even established his own factory for making paper.

As postmaster general he came to appreciate the vast potential for mail circulation. His success in popularizing his almanac outside Pennsylvania to the other colonies revealed his talent for mass merchandising. In a day when prices were what the market could bear, Franklin believed that low prices spelled volume and bigger profits.

CITY FATHER

Although William Penn laid out Philadelphia, it was Franklin's innovations that made the second-largest city in the British Empire a safer place to live. He was the first to dispatch constables or policemen on regular beats. He also established a fire department and invented a new kind of streetlight.

DIPLOMAT

Franklin was America's first diplomat. He sailed from Philadelphia to France in 1776 to open a U.S. ministry in Versailles. He succeeded in persuading France to loan the insolvent American Continental Congress the thousands of francs necessary to keep the Continental Army in the field. When that was accomplished, Franklin returned home.

In 1782 he again assumed diplomatic duties as U.S. commissioner, helping to successfully negotiate the Treaty of Paris to conclude the war with Britain.

ECONOMIST

Franklin was America's first political economist. Like Adam Smith, his contemporary in Scotland, he opposed tariffs and government subsidies. It was Franklin who popularized in this country the phrase *laissez-faire,* which he adopted from Smith, whom he met and discussed ideas with. Franklin was also an anti-imperialist: He opposed mercantilism or state control of economic policy.

EDITOR

In his day Franklin was the giant among American editors. He was the editor of his newspaper, the Pennsylvania *Gazette,* as well as the publisher and editor of the almanac. As a newspaper editor, he introduced planted spicy news items (some invented) and the editorial as the opinion piece of a newspaper.

EDUCATOR

In life he established the Philadelphia Academy, which became the College of Philadelphia. Now it is known as the University of Pennsylvania. In death he provided trust funds to further the education of young men in Boston and Philadelphia.

Although he himself had but two years of formal schooling, he was a believer in education. His library of over four thousand books was the largest private library in America at the time. As he himself wrote, he chose printing as a trade to be next to books. He was also the father of the first circulating library in America.

In one essay in 1782, "Proposals Relating to the Education of Youth in Pennsylvania," Franklin sketched out his idea of a college. He proposed not only teachers and a library, but also a campus that included a science laboratory as well as acres for agricultural experiments and fields for playing games. Since physical exercise, in Franklin's view, should also include swimming, he recommended that the campus be located next to a lake or river.

ENVIRONMENTALIST

Franklin was America's first environmentalist. He was an advocate of conservation and a foe of pollution. He inveighed against the wholesale stripping of forests and the fouling of rivers with wastes. One specific example was Franklin's plea for an end to the waste that tanneries emptied into Dock Creek, a tributary of the Delaware in Philadelphia.

FEMINIST

As a sixteen-year-old in Boston, Franklin penned anonymous letters under the name of Silence Dogood. Mistress Dogood was purportedly a widow lady who ran her late husband's shop. In her letters she contended that women could not only run businesses better, but also could just as well excel as lawyers, doctors, and preachers. The Puritan city fathers deemed such views scandalous.

FOUNDING FATHER

Franklin was the most productive Founding Father. He was the only one who signed the five charter documents of the United States.

GENERAL

Because of its Quaker hegemony, Pennsylvania was slow to prepare a military defense. Franklin prepared a do-it-yourself kit for counties to raise their own militias. The formula was to make it a "club," with the price of admittance the purchase of one's own musket. If a member was late for drill, he paid a fine, which was used to buy a cannon. The result of his quickly assembled army of militiamen in Pennsylvania's counties was a generalship for Franklin.

In 1756, after Braddock's disastrous defeat in western Pennsylvania by the French, General Franklin was called into action as the very existence of the largest English colony was imperiled. Franklin led a march up the Delaware to shore up defenses. He built Fort Allen and organized the German Moravian settlers in the defense of Bethlehem, Pennsylvania.

GOVERNOR

After Franklin returned from his diplomatic duties in Versailles in 1777, he took the lead in drafting a new constitution for the Commonwealth of Pennsylvania. Under that charter, he was elected president of the Executive Council, or governor. He served three years.

INVENTOR

Next to his trade of printing, Franklin is best known for his hobby of inventing. Bifocal glasses, the Franklin stove, the lightning rod, and the armonica are just some of his inventions.

JUDGE

In 1751 Franklin sat as presiding judge or justice of the peace involving cases of assault, larceny, and contract disputes. He resigned because he felt he had insufficient knowledge of the common law.

LADIES' MAN

Franklin is wrongly pictured as a womanizer, but women did find him charming. In no small way, it may have been because he was a feminist who respected the intelligence and worth of women. In a day when few women had more than a few years of schooling, women's opinions on matters other than the home were little respected. Franklin was an exception. After all, he also had little formal education.

In addition, Franklin, unlike other eighteenth-century men whose favorite conversational topics were hunting and horses, could talk about the methods of cooking and the craft of spinning cotton and wool, or about ideas for household improvements. Franklin was a collector of herbs and designed for the home a cold-storage pantry for vegetables. Yet his most endearing gift to the women in his life was his sense of humor, particularly the rare gift—in his day—of laughing at himself.

LEGISLATOR
After twelve years as the clerk of the Pennsylvania General Assembly, Franklin at age forty entered his name as a candidate for the State House. He was elected and served off and on for twenty years. Some of his main legislative initiatives were appropriations for hospitals and education.

LINGUIST
Although Franklin had only two years of schooling, he taught himself to speak French, Spanish, and Italian. It was said that one reason Franklin was chosen by the Continental Congress to be the U.S. envoy to France was that he was the only American to speak French!

LOBBYIST
Franklin was America's first lobbyist. He was paid by the Pennsylvania General Assembly to persuade the British Parliament

to eliminate or decrease the taxes on the colonies. Later Delaware, New Jersey, and Georgia retained his services. His efforts resulted in repealing the Stamp Act, but he failed to convince the British government that the continued heavy taxation of the colonies would lead to American rebellion.

MASON

Franklin was a Mason who belonged to the Philadelphia Lodge and became its grand master in 1734. That same year he published the first Masonic book in America: *The Constitutions of the Free Masons*. In France he would attend lodge meetings with Europe's most famous Mason, Voltaire.

MUSICIAN

Franklin played the harp, guitar, and violin, and invented the armonica. He also was a ballad writer.

NEWSPAPER PUBLISHER

Franklin was the founder and editor of the Pennsylvania *Gazette* while only in his twenties. He was simultaneously the sole reporter, editor, typesetter, printer, circulation man, and business manager. As reporter, he covered the governor's office and news from abroad.

NUTRITIONIST

Franklin was America's first nutritionist. Although he was not a vegetarian, he did recommend a sparing menu of red meat. Instead he advocated fish and fowl such as chicken and turkey (but not duck, because it was too fatty). He believed most Americans ate themselves to death. Accordingly, he championed the idea of a light supper. A lover of vegetables, he also advocated the eating of fruit to eliminate scurvy in a balanced diet.

PHILOSOPHER

Herman Melville, the writer of *Moby Dick,* referred to Franklin as "a household Plato." Franklin, however, was a utilitarian and not a theorist. Yet as America's most famous product of the Age of Reason, he insisted that action be based on reason. Like many free thinkers in the eighteenth century, he was repelled by the dark notions of inherent evil preached by theologians. Franklin reveled in "the pursuit of happiness," but such joy came not from pleasure but from satisfying work that gave one a sense of fulfillment.

POLITICAL SCIENTIST

Although Franklin poked fun at academicians, he put his own theories of government into practice. He drew up the abortive Albany Plan to unite the colonies in 1757. He wrote the first U.S. charter—the Articles of Confederation. He also drafted, in 1777, the Constitution of Pennsylvania, which introduced the idea in America of the unicameral legislature.

POSTMASTER GENERAL

Franklin is America's most famous postmaster. As postmaster general for the colonies, he established post offices in all the thirteen colonies. As colonial postmaster general, he cut the time of mailing from Philadelphia to Boston from six weeks to six days. He also pioneered the idea of a dead letter office.

PRINTER

Despite his other accomplishments, whether it be legislating in the Pennsylvania General Assembly, lobbying in Parliament in London, or negotiating in his diplomatic duties in France, Franklin always introduced himself as "Ben Franklin, printer."

Franklin once said he was a member of no class because he was a member of all classes. As a printer, he'd say, "I work with my hands, so I'm working class." But as the owner of the shop, he'd add, "I'm a businessman, so I'm a member of the middle class. And as a writer," he'd continue, "I guess I might qualify as educated or upper class."

PROPAGANDIST

During the Revolutionary War, Franklin concocted disinformation in Paris to turn sentiment against the English. He had bills of lading printed up for shipments of American scalps that purported to be accounts receivable presented for payment to the British by the Iroquois allies of the English.

He also leaked a fake letter by a Hessian count to a German general in charge of the German principality's mercenaries fighting for George III. The letter urged the general to employ the Hessian hirelings as cannon fodder. Advising the general not to spoil them with generous stipends, the count's letter urged glorifying death as "a Hero's highest reward." The letter had the effect of discouraging German recruits.

PUBLIC RELATIONS WIZARD

Franklin would understand today's photo opportunity to create news. He invented the idea behind it. When he first arrived at the

French court, he wore a beaver fur hat, plain clothes, and no wig—which he knew would stand out among the satin, velvet, and powdered wigs of French courtiers. Franklin knew he was making a statement.

His sketch of the cartoon snake in pieces with the caption "Unite or Die" was so popular it led to the "Don't Tread on Me" emblems on the early flags for independence.

The switch of his postal frank as Postmaster General from "B. Franklin . . . FREE" to "B. FREE . . . Franklin" was another ploy to build support for the cause of independence.

Imagination, wit, and a keen understanding of human nature made him a natural in public relations. His achievements in diplomacy and productive fund-raising owe much to his skill in public relations.

SCIENTIST

Franklin was the colonies' most prominent scientist. His curious mind made him ever a seeker, probing nature's mysteries. He established the American Philosophical Society, whose treatises were mostly in the realm of natural philosophy—as theoretical science was often called in the eighteenth century.

Franklin's published findings on electricity in lightning were the first in the world. Franklin also investigated the causes and phenomena of the aurora borealis and discovered the Gulf Stream.

One example of his interest in biology was the glass "body" he kept in his house displaying the veins and arteries. His experiments led him to be the first American elected to the Royal Society in London.

SONGWRITER

Franklin was one of the colonies' most successful songwriters. An irrepressible versifier, he started to pen lyrics for tavern drinking songs in his early days at Philadelphia.

One of his first went:

Fair Venus call on her voice obey
In beauty's arms spend night and day
The joys of love all joys excel
And loving's certainly doing well.

Another was:

'Twas old Noah first planted the vine
And mended his morals by drinking to wine
He justly the drinking of water decried
For he knew that all mankind by drinking of, died.

Franklin would pen scores of songs in his life. One of his last was one in French called *"Ça Tiendra"* (It will catch on) he composed while in Paris.

SWIMMING TEACHER

Franklin was not only an advocate of swimming as physical exercise to maintain the body, he even gave swimming lessons when he was a young man in Philadelphia. As an old man of eighty in France, he swam across the Seine River in Paris.

THEOLOGIAN

Franklin espoused a primitive and pristine Christianity shorn of baptism and religious rites. To Franklin, there was no need of a church edifice. A deist, he wrote to the president of Yale six weeks before his death, "I believe in one God, Creator of the Universe in that He ought to be worshiped . . . that the soul of man is immortal."

In Franklin's credo, to love God was to do good to man. Jesus was not the Son of God but the supreme example of man.

Franklin also rewrote parts of the Bible in clearer English. The rewriting was scorned by religious authorities.

Anecdotes and Adventures

After a century dominated by gloomy theologians, Franklin seemed to arrive like a bright chuckle after a stern sermon. In Boston, from which Franklin hailed, the Puritan city fathers did not appreciate a joke. In the seventeenth-century city, people in Boston described as "impish" and "devilish" were not subjects of mirth but candidates for the punishing stocks.

Franklin found a more congenial home in Philadelphia. But his love of funny stories, penchant for pranks, and flair for spoofs and satire distinguished him from his contemporaries. The one stereotype Americans conjure up of Franklin is that of merry old Ben—a kind of wise and jolly Saint Nick without the beard or red costume.

Compare Franklin with the sternly visaged General George Washington from Virginia or the dour John Adams, Franklin's co-commissioner in the Paris peace talks, who was unamused by Franklin's frolics in France. Personalities such as Washington, Adams, or "the radical Tom Paine" spawned few funny anecdotes.

It was said in 1776 that Franklin was not asked to write the Declaration of Independence because he might insert a joke in it. Almost the same thing was said a century later about Abraham Lincoln: Planners for the Gettysburg ceremony balked at inviting him to deliver remarks at the cemetery in 1863 because they feared he would try to say something funny.

Franklin was the first in the great American tradition of raconteurs. Abraham Lincoln, Mark Twain, Lyndon Johnson, Senator Sam Ervin, and Senator Everett Dirksen, who would follow in his wake, were all splendid spinners of tall tales.

It is a distinct genre of American humor that developed in its early days, when a traveler felt he had to "sing for his supper" in his host's home. Franklin would perfect the art of telling an anecdote to illustrate a point. Such was not the habit of eighteenth-century English gentlemen. British humor—particularly that which emanated from the London coffeehouses and parliamentary lobbies—featured the quick riposte and clever wordplay. British humor was often subtle and understated, while American storytelling was broad, bawdy, and exaggerated. If British humor was scholarly, and replete with literary allusions, the American brand that Franklin wielded drew its inspiration from the earthy vernacular of the men on the street.

The cruel jibe or savage retort was also not part of Franklin's nature. The aim of his storytelling, like Lincoln's a century later, was to diffuse tension or prove a point. Franklin's comic versifying in the almanac would have been scorned by the genteel readers of London's *Spectator*. In the partisan magazines or in the competitive spirit of Parliament, laughter was always at the expense of someone.

Franklin came not from the educated but the working classes, among whom beer songs, not books, provided light relief. Similarly, the pranks Franklin liked to play were part of this folkish fun. The tastes of British aristocrats, on the other hand, ran to masques and more organized skits.

From his anonymous penning of the Silence Dogood letters in Puritan Boston to his printing up of fake sales slips for selling of scalps in France fifty-five years later, Franklin relished the spoof. In a day when pomposity in preachers, pedagogues, and politicians seemed a virtue, Franklin took delight in deflating the conceited and poking fun at pretense. Yet, unlike many wits, Franklin also enjoyed a laugh at his own expense.

Many of the stories I have collected over the years cannot be absolutely verified. No doubt some are apocryphal. As a Philadelphian, I have heard stories of Franklin's wit and humor that have been passed down for generations. Some of the anecdotes, of course, came from his own writings.

Franklin once said he would like to have lived in this century. If a time machine could have arranged that for him, he would have found that his humor would still evoke laughter from today's listeners. Franklin is funny—whatever the century.

તા તા તા

AGE BEFORE BEAUTY

If Benjamin Franklin was an author of liberty, he was also an authority on love. To young men he would recommend the advantages of older women for liaisons. He would say:

They don't tell
They don't yell
They don't swell
And they're grateful as hell!

"ALL WORK AND NO PLAGIARIZING MAKE SAM A DULL BOY"

Franklin was not regular in his attendance at the First Presbyterian Church in Philadelphia. He did not care for the long discourses on predestination that usually emanated from the pulpit.

He resumed his churchgoing when a young preacher named Samuel Hemphill arrived from England. Hemphill, who was a welcome refreshment from the dour dogma usually heard, delivered lively homilies on the need for good works in daily life.

When attendance increased, other, more conservative preachers in the presbytery began to examine closely Hemphill's sermons. They found that he had been lifting his discourses from a book of sermons published in London.

At a hearing, Franklin came to the young preacher's defense. "I'd rather hear good sermons composed by others than the bad ones of the preacher before."

Privately he confided, "Better a good plagiarist than a dull Calvinist."

ANIMAL HUSBAND-RY!

If not the first feminist, Franklin was the first prominent American to be sensitive to the concerns of women.

Franklin in a conversation said that for some women, wifedom was a form of slavery or worse. He told of an ocean crossing when a ship, because of bad weather, sought shelter in Jamaica.

That night, as a storm raged across the island, the innkeeper roused his frail wife from her sickbed to go out and purchase some provisions.

Franklin, noting a young and robust black woman who was waiting on them, asked the owner why he didn't send her out instead of his wife.

The innkeeper answered, "The slave girl I bought for sixty pounds. I'm not going to risk my investment in her. But if my wife dies, that's no financial loss. In fact, if I marry again, I might gain some extra pounds in her dowry."

APPOINTMENT AND DIS-APPOINTMENT

John Hancock, the president of the Continental Congress, welcomed Benjamin Franklin back from England in 1775 with the news, "Dr. Franklin, we're giving you your old job back as postmaster general of the Colonies."

Franklin chuckled. "I never seek, I never refuse, I never resign an office."

AS DIFFERENT AS BLACK AND WHITE

Franklin was a deist. In a nutshell, a deist believed in God but not in the divinity of Christ. On one occasion, a critic, referring to Franklin's religious views, called him an atheist. Franklin replied, "No, I'm a deist. Calling me an atheist is like picking up a piece of chalk and calling it charcoal."

AT THE END OF MY ROPE

In 1774 Franklin had grown weary of his mission as the American colonial agent. In London his enemies said he took bribes from American merchants to impede British exports. Back home, reports circulated that he was about to accept a knighthood from George III for his connivance with the Tory government.

Reconciliation with the mother country seemed impossible. A creative man by bent, Franklin found that he was tired of reading tax bills and drafting legislative alternatives. In fact, he was tired of talking about taxes.

He told an American visitor to London, "I've begun to feel like the sailor on shipboard when he was pulling a heavy cable from the shore leave.

"A mate sighed, saying, ''Tis a long, long cable. I wish I could see the end of it.'

"'Damn it,' replied the first sailor, 'if it ever had an end, somebody cut it off!'"

"AY, THERE'S THE CATCH"

At a Philadelphia tavern Franklin was listening to friends discuss the Declaration of Independence. From another table, a young fellow who had been overserved with rum tottered toward Franklin's chair. "Aw, them words don't mean nothin' a-tall!" he shouted at Franklin. "Where's all the happiness that document says it guarantees us?"

Franklin smiled benevolently at the questioner and quickly replied, "My friend, the declaration only guarantees the American people the right to pursue happiness. You have to catch it yourself!"

THE "AYES" AND THE WISE

If the French aristocracy were elated by the American colonies' rebellion against Britain, they were less than enthusiastic about the American form of government.

At a dinner in Paris with Franklin, one French count ridiculed the idea of letting the educated elite be ruled by the uneducated majority.

The count challenged, "All those who say yes to the idea that the ignorant majority should not govern the wise minority, rise from the table and follow me to the salon."

All rose to depart. Franklin, who remained at the table, quipped, "Gentlemen, I must be the wise minority."

BAD DAD

While Franklin awaited the birth of his grandchild, he told his son-in-law of a visitor who had complained that a midwife had charged him double the fee that she had received from a neighbor of his.

Franklin sought out the woman.

"Dr. Franklin, I reckon he's right. You see, when his baby arrived, he asked me, 'What did I get, boy or a girl?' Now, if he asked me, 'How's my missus?' I would have charged him only half the amount."

"BILLY, I HARDLY KNEW YE"

Franklin's relationship with his illegitimate son William was always strained, even though he reared William in his Philadelphia home with the blessing of his wife Deborah. (In fact, Franklin would later adopt William's illegitimate child, Temple Franklin, as his grandson, and Temple would live with Franklin in London.)

William Franklin was appointed royal governor of New Jersey by George III. Perhaps because of his tainted lineage, young Franklin was all the more susceptible to the perquisites of royal office.

When Franklin returned to Philadelphia in 1775, his daughter Sarah gave him the distressing news, "Billy is a Tory."

Franklin immediately went to Trenton to talk with his governor son. It has been said that he warned, "Billy, if you choose the king as your master, you may lose me as a father." William Franklin did side with the king and a rupture in their relations was the result.

THE BISHOP AND THE BEGGAR

As the colonial agent in London, Franklin wearied of the British government's flimsy assurances and empty promises. When Tory ministers offered to consider the question of taxes and the ban against American exports, Franklin recounted this story of the alms-seeking mendicant.

Outside the cathedral, a beggar held his cup out for churchgoers. Then the bishop, resplendent in his cassock robes, appeared.

"Please give me a pound, Your Grace," the poor man pleaded. The bishop said no.

"Perhaps maybe a shilling, then," the wretch implored. The prelate again shook his head.

"Then how about either a tuppenny or a benediction?"

"Well," beamed the bishop, "I will gladly offer a blessing."

"Forget it," said the beggar. "If you're that anxious to offer a prayer, it's not worth even a tuppenny."

A BLACKENED REPUTATION

Robert Hunter landed in Philadelphia in 1767 to be sworn in as the commonwealth's new governor. Among the very first people he invited to the governor's mansion was Pennsylvania's most famous citizen, who had just returned from one of his sojourns in London. Hunter had been selected by King George III and not by the

Proprietors, and Franklin, no friend of the Proprietary "party," supported the change.

Because of the political controversy attending the appointment, Hunter asked Franklin his views on selecting a governor.

Franklin jokingly replied, "I always like what Sancho Panza, Don Quixote's squire, said about choosing a governor to rule. He said, 'I'd pick a slave because I could sell him if he proved to be no good.'"

Hunter replied, "But I don't have a black face."

"Yes," said Franklin, who had observed some tyrannous behavior of previous governors. "But in due time your name, if not your face, will be blackened."

"BLESSED ARE THE POOR . . ."

At the Constitutional Convention no delegate was more fearful of the dangers of democracy than Gouverneur Morris. A monarchist by conviction, the patrician Philadelphian had been a late convert to the patriot cause in the recent War for Independence.

When those like Franklin pleaded for giving a wider franchise of voting rights to the people, Morris's face would turn almost the color of his mahogany peg leg.

At one point, it is said, during a convention debate Morris unscrewed his wooden leg and pounded it on the pew bench.

"It is no use giving the vote to the poor—they will only sell it to the rich!"

Franklin stared directly at Morris and replied, "It wasn't the poor who gave those fancy balls that winter in Philadelphia for English officers—was it? And it wasn't the rich that same winter who froze with General Washington at Valley Forge."

BLESSED EVENT-UALITY

As a boy, Franklin was given only a few pennies for the work helping his father. One day, when the eight-year-old had come home from school, his father asked what he had learned that day.

Franklin replied, "the Beatitudes."

"How many are there?" quizzed his father.

"Nine," answered Franklin, "but there should be ten like the Commandments."

"Ten?" questioned his father. "What do you say should be the tenth?"

Franklin's impish answer was, "Blessed are they who have the means to give to those who need it."

BLOW ONE'S TOP?

In the drafty days before central heating, people—particularly those of the older generation—were accustomed to wearing caps indoors to warm their heads.

A younger associate visited Franklin at his Philadelphia house and was surprised to find the balding old man at his desk with a cap not on his head but laying aside on the desk.

"Dr. Franklin," the associate asked, "why aren't you wearing your cap?"

"My head gets warm," replied Franklin.

"Oh, Dr. Franklin," the young man countered, referring to the noted equability of the Philadelphia sage and philosopher, "no one could ever call you a hothead."

"Well, God must think so," Franklin said with a chuckle, "since he has removed the hair from my head."

BORED STIFF

At the Constitutional Convention the most articulate advocate for monarchy was the young Alexander Hamilton. Franklin, who fervently opposed the idea of an American monarch, nevertheless urged Hamilton to deliver an academic discourse to the delegates citing Athenian and Roman precedents with quotations in Greek and Latin from his authoritative sources. Hamilton, encouraged by Franklin, pontificated to the delegates for an hour on the philosophical merits of monarchy.

It was said that some delegates came to Franklin and remonstrated, "We understand that you asked Hamilton to make the speech."

"Yes," replied Franklin dryly. "Those who were not scared to death were bored to death!"

As Franklin predicted, the idea of monarchy was delivered a swift execution by the delegates.

"BRANDY IS DANDY . . ."

In London Franklin was challenged by English leaders who were angered by the colonial protests to the paying of new taxes. Franklin countered by saying that remonstrance is better than rebellion.

To illustrate his point, he told the story of a man who came to him for advice complaining that his neighbors were tapping into the keg of beer that he kept in the backyard.

Franklin told him, "If you want to stop your neighbors from drinking your beer, put a vat of brandy beside it and they won't touch the beer."

The moral, said Franklin, was, "If you British offer us the brandy of home rule, our stealing away of your tax revenue will cease."

BUMPS IN THE NIGHT

Shortly after he set himself up as a printer in Philadelphia, Franklin returned home to visit his parents. While in Boston he called on the famous theologian Cotton Mather, whose sermons thundered from his pulpit in the late seventeenth and early eighteenth centuries. Late in the evening when they needed some refreshments, the old preacher asked Franklin to go to the cellar. "Be careful," warned Mather, "the ceilings are low." Despite the admonition, Franklin bumped his head.

Mather, hearing the cry from Franklin, went to him. Franklin was shaken but not seriously hurt.

"Ben," Mather intoned, "you will encounter many bumps in life. You must always remember to duck."

Mather may be known for his theological sermons of predestination, but those words "to duck" Franklin would often cite as his life's motto and philosophy of not looking for trouble.

CART BEFORE THE HORSE

In Paris one night the discussion at the table turned to the Bible's Ten Commandments. Franklin once said that in addition, there are two other precepts.

"First," said Franklin, "we are told to increase and multiply and replenish the earth.

"Later," he continued, "we are commanded to love one another.

"I have always thought," opined Franklin drolly, "there was an editorial mix-up in the taking down of God's words—surely the order of those two precepts should have been reversed."

CHINESE PUZZLE

Franklin once chided an English scientist for his findings. His conclusions, Franklin told him, were undermined by his failure to do the necessary preliminary tests.

Franklin said he was reminded of a Philadelphia merchant who received a case of vermilion slabs with straps in a shipment from China. He immediately assumed the slabs were Chinese shoes and began arguing which end of the shoe was the front and which was the back.

A woman who entered the store looked at the strapped piece and said, "Gentlemen, are you sure it really is a shoe? Isn't that the first question to be decided?"

CITY OF BROTHERLY LOVE?

In France, Franklin received the news that General Washington's Continental Army had suffered a disastrous defeat at the hands of General Howe at the Battle of Brandywine twenty-five miles southwest of Philadelphia on the Delaware border.

A French leader voiced his fear to the American envoy. "Dr. Franklin, General Howe will next conquer Philadelphia."

Franklin, thinking of all the balls and banquets the buxom belles of Philadelphia's Tory elite would stage for redcoat officers, replied, "No, it will be Philadelphia that will conquer the British."

CUP AND SAUCER

At the Constitutional Convention Franklin initially pushed for one legislative chamber based on population. Yet when the convention deadlocked between the populous states and the less populous ones, he came around to the idea of having both a House and a Senate as a compromise.

To those delegates who questioned this idea of having two legislative houses, Franklin told a tale about a man who had recently visited General Washington in Philadelphia. The visitor, when taking coffee, filled his saucer with it before pouring it into his cup. When the general asked him why, the visitor answered, "To cool off the coffee." And Washington replied, "That's why we need a Senate—the Senate is the saucer: It can cool off what the House cooks up!"

DECLINE AND FALL

Before the Revolutionary War, Benjamin Franklin lobbied in London for revisions of Parliament's tax laws. He paid visits to fellow writers whose views might be more sympathetic to the American position. Franklin called on the eminent historian Edward Gibbon, who had just completed his monumental work *The Decline and Fall of the Roman Empire*. Gibbon, however, wouldn't receive him, saying from the other side of the door, "I decline to associate with anyone who would dishonor my king."

Franklin answered back, "That's a pity—because you'll soon be writing a sequel—*Decline and Fall of the British Empire*."

DIE HAPPY

One of Franklin's newspaper competitors won circulation by its vitriolic assassination of leading Pennsylvania figures. Yet when the subjects of his attack died, the editor would compensate by penning glowing testaments to their characters.

When Franklin ran across his publishing rival one day, he chided him, "I read that obituary in your paper yesterday. You always seem to give our leading Pennsylvania citizens, while living, characters of the devil, but when they die they suddenly turn into angels. When one of them dies, it is always delightful to read what a good husband, good father, good citizen, and a good Christian he was and then you culminate your eulogy with some lofty lines of poetry that certainly enshrine him for heavenly admittance.

"So I think Pennsylvania is a bad place to live but a good place to die in!"

"DO-GOODER"

In the 1720s, Puritan Boston was shocked by the writings of Mistress Silence Dogood. The author claimed to be a widow who was running her late husband's shop at better profit than he had in his business life.

Her essays, published in James Franklin's New England *Courant,* also spread the scandalous idea that women could practice with success the professions of law, medicine, and ministry.

The Puritan city fathers called James Franklin and asked him who this "Mistress Dogood" was. James Franklin answered that he would find the letters from Mistress Dogood under his door when he arrived on Monday morning.

The next Monday, James Franklin arrived early. When he noticed the packet coming in under the door, he opened it. To his surprise, it was his young brother Ben. Ben, while serving as apprentice to his older brother, had been the letters' mysterious author.

"Ben," James thundered, "you're fired. It's back to making candles for Father. As an apprentice, don't you realize you are virtually my slave for the next six years?"

The seventeen-year-old Franklin answered, "I will be a slave to no one—not even my brother," and soon left for Philadelphia. A half century later he would not be a slave—not even to the mother country, England.

DUNKARDS, NOT DULLARDS!

The Dunkards are a plainly clothed religious sect who came to Pennsylvania from the Palatinate region of Germany. They are closely related to the Amish and Mennonites.

A leader of the group came to Franklin to ask his advice on how to stop the vicious rumors that were being spread about them. Their quaint custom of "bundling" was being smeared as "wife-sharing" and incest.

Franklin, who was a printer by trade, naturally suggested that it might be well for them to publish their articles of belief in order to stop the talk.

The Dunkard pastor demurred. "Oh, no," he replied, "we couldn't do that—we never know when God will reveal to us new truths."

Franklin exclaimed in response, "Imagine a church having a dogma that's not dogmatic!"

DUPLICATE DOPES

At the time of the Townsend Tax Bill, a British minister cited the example of the Spanish government exacting taxes from the Netherlands before they gained their independence.

Franklin exclaimed in disgust, "The British ministers read history not to escape blunders but to copy them."

EMBRACEABLE YOU!

At the time of the War for Independence, there was a rakish member of the House of Commons named John Wilkes. Wilkes took delight in supporting Benjamin Franklin and the American cause, much to the consternation of the Tory government. Wilkes was also a member of a bacchanalian revelers' group named the Hell-Fire Club.

One day, after a speech that seemed treasonable to the Tory hierarchy, Wilkes found himself attacked by a member of the front bench, Lord Sandwich. Sandwich said, "The honorable gentleman who consorts with the traitor and rogue Franklin will have a limited career in this chamber, for it shall either end on the gallows or by a loathsome disease."

Wilkes coolly replied, "The Honorable Lord may well be correct. It all depends on whether I embrace His Lordship's programs or his mistress."

THE END AND THE BEGINNING

Though Franklin, while worshiping in Philadelphia, remained a nominal Presbyterian, he held the city's dominant Quaker faith in high esteem for their absence of doctrine and ritual. When a visitor from England expressed interest in the religion, Franklin took him to a Friends meeting.

After sitting down, the Anglican fidgeted restlessly during the silence. When ten minutes passed, he whispered to Franklin, "When does the service begin?"

Franklin replied, "The service begins when the meeting ends."

ERECTOR SET

At the Constitutional Convention, Franklin opposed the proposed provision for a standing army. Remembering the abuses the king's troops inflicted on the colonials, Franklin worried that it would be like "a president's police force." He argued that any armed forces should be authorized annually by vote of Congress. Franklin helped defeat the army provision in conversations with delegates by offering this analogy: "A standing army is like an erect member. While it does enhance domestic harmony and conjugal bliss, it may also invite temptation and foreign adventures."

EXCUSE ME

A young man who sought an appointment with Franklin failed to show up at the scheduled time at the printer's shop. The next day the job seeker came to see Franklin and offered an elaborate explanation involving an ailing aunt.

Franklin dismissed him, saying, "A man who is good at making an excuse is seldom good at anything else."

"THE 'EYES' HAVE IT!"

In France, Ambassador Franklin was hailed as "the man who seized lightning from the heavens." At a royal reception, Louis XVI's young and beautiful queen flirted with the older Franklin. Batting her lustrous eyes, Marie Antoinette said, "Dr. Franklin, aren't you aware of the fate of Prometheus, who was tortured to death for the crime of stealing the fire from Jove?"

Franklin replied, "If creating sparks is a crime, your eyes cause more mischief in a night than all my experiments of a lifetime."

FAG RAG

In colonial days, tailors and merchants of clothing used to call the scraps left from their making of breeches and coats "fag ends." They would dump them into a basket and sell the fag ends for any price they could get.

When the Continental Congress appointed Franklin at the age of seventy-one to be the U.S. envoy to Paris in 1777, his friend Dr. Benjamin Rush implored the aged Philadelphian not to leave for such a difficult voyage and stressful assignment.

Franklin replied with a sad smile, "I am old and good for nothing—I'm like what the storekeepers say of their remnants of cloth—a fag end. So to the Continental Congress I say I am a fag end. You may have me for whatever use you can find for me."

FEATHER VAIN?

In Paris a mademoiselle repeated to Franklin a compliment that King Louis XVI had made about the American envoy.

"Dr. Franklin," she purred, "that must be a feather in your hat."

"A feather in my hat," replied Franklin, "is like the pretty silk garters you wear under your petticoats. No, on second thought," added Franklin, "a garter at least performs the function of holding up your hose."

FLAT BROKE

Franklin as U.S. minister to France was a popular sensation. A fashionable piece of jewelry was a Wedgwood blue jasperware cameo of his likeness which duchesses, countesses, and other titled ladies of France wore as a pendant on their low-cut gowns.

At one reception, King Louis noticed one rather thin lady who came up to purr over Franklin. When she left, the king commented, "It's a pity, Franklin, she does not do justice to her décolletage. God did not endow her."

"Yes," said Franklin, "but you, sire, on the other hand, can endow us. For our government in Philadelphia, like the unfortunate lady in question, has the same problem—an uncovered deficit."

FREEZE-OUT

In the winter of 1752 when the French invaded Pennsylvania, Franklin traveled up the Delaware River to Bethlehem to supervise the building of a fort. The first night in Bethlehem he stayed in a rooming house. As he inspected his feather bed, he observed that the sheets were damp. He asked the landlady if she would air the bed linens.

After supper, he retired. When he lay down, the sheets were icy slabs.

A frozen Franklin descended the stairs to confront his hostess.

"Mr. Franklin, I aired them just as you asked."

"How did you air them?" asked her guest.

"Why, I laid them out to dry right on those hedges just outside the house."

GETTING THE HANG OF IT

At the time of the signing of the Declaration of Independence, the president of the Continental Congress, John Hancock, was the first to sign. As Hancock leaned over the table to inscribe his signature, he said to Franklin, "I'm writing it large so that George III can see it without his spectacles." Letting the ink dry, he added, "We must be unanimous. There must be no pulling different ways; we must all hang together."

"Yes," Franklin agreed, "we must indeed all hang together, or most assuredly we will all hang separately."

GOLDEN HANDSHAKE

The Royal Society in London presented Franklin with its prestigious Gold Medal in 1767. The society was drawn from the elite ranks of the greatest scientists, university scholars, and literary giants. Their award to Franklin was singular for two reasons: Franklin was not only the first American, but the first tradesman and non-university graduate so honored.

After the presentation was made, Franklin told the banquet guests, "For centuries the scientists of your society have searched for that formula in alchemy which would turn cruder metal into gold. I don't know whether any of you have ever succeeded in that quest to create gold, but you mastered the art of making a piece of gold infinitely more valuable."

"GRIN AND BEAR IT"

Only the reigning monarchs of the day had their portraits painted more than Benjamin Franklin. Yet Franklin begrudged the time he had to pose, which robbed him of hours he could spend on his experiments, studies, or business duties.

While Franklin was in London as the agent of the Pennsylvania Colony, one of the most celebrated eighteenth-century artists in London, the American Benjamin West, came to sketch a Franklin portrait.

"Mr. West," warned Franklin, "if you want to catch me in a happy mood, do it fast. I don't sit too well too long."

HALF WIT

At the beginning of the French and Indian War, the British troops under General Braddock were amassing in Pennsylvania to fight the French, who held Fort Duquesne (now Pittsburgh), which was the gateway to the Ohio Valley. Braddock was irate at what he felt was the American reluctance to give backup support to his Redcoat troops.

As postmaster general, Franklin was considered to be the best troubleshooter. So he was asked to go to Carlisle to meet Braddock.

When Franklin arrived in Carlisle, he interrupted an argument that Braddock was having with a tall young colonel of the Virginia Militia named George Washington. Braddock was incensed that the German farmers of Pennsylvania would not give him their wagons to help the British fight the French. With his face as red as his tunic, Braddock fumed to Washington, "I have half a mind to take those wagons from those Germans at the point of a musket."

Franklin interjected with a smile, "Well, General, you're right about one thing—your mind!"

HAND SIGNALS

A young minister named Samuel Hemphill had been dismissed by the First Presbyterian Church of Philadelphia. Franklin had liked the young parson's spirited homilies, but unfortunately it was discovered that Hemphill had plagiarized his sermons. When a co-congregant asked Franklin his opinion of the disgraced minister, Franklin said, "Except for his failure to punctuate, his discourses were flawless."

"Punctuation?" queried his friend.

"Yes." Franklin smiled. "He forgot to put up two fingers when he began his sermon and his two left fingers when he concluded— the quotation marks."

THE HAT TRICK

Franklin once called on a rich Quaker friend who lived all by himself in an enormous house. As Franklin walked through the rooms of the mansion, he said, "Sir, why do you go to the cost of keeping up this immense house when you just need a fraction of the space?"

The rich man replied, "I have the means."

Upon entering the dining room, Franklin saw a table that could seat twenty-five people. He asked, "Why such a large table?"

The wealthy man again answered, "I have the means."

"In that case," said Franklin, taking the hat from the Quaker's head, "why don't you have a hat big enough for twenty-five people? You have the means!"

HEEDLESS HORSEMAN

When George III succeeded his grandfather as king in 1760, he was viewed with high hopes.

At the very beginning of his reign, even Franklin was optimistic about the young king, but soon his expectations were dashed by his bullheaded policies.

As the king's policy on taxation grew more oppressive, Franklin lamented the inevitable split in relations the Crown's policies would lead to.

While Franklin watched with a friend the young and handsomely attired king ride on horseback in the ceremonies for the opening of Parliament one year, his friend offered this defense of George III: "Well, he is a fine-figured king and he's the first British monarch in almost half a century to speak English."

"Well," answered Franklin, "that doesn't help with his speech impediment."

"Speech impediment!" was the startled response.

"Yes," said Franklin. "He doesn't listen!"

HELL-BENT

As George Washington's Continental Army suffered a succession of reverses in the field, the French government wavered on its policy to support the Americans. The French indecision frustrated Minister Franklin.

When a French official asked Franklin if he thought America was headed for inevitable defeat, Franklin shook his head and offered a story of the Catholic who questioned a Presbyterian preacher.

"Parson, do you believe in prejudgment?"

The minister nodded assent.

The Catholic continued, "You mean, Parson, you really subscribe to the tenets of foreordainment?"

"Yes," the minister answered.

"You agree," the Catholic pressed further, "with the doctrine of predestination!"

"Well," replied the minister, "I'd rather be a Presbyterian knowing I'm going to hell than a Catholic not knowing where the hell I'm going."

A HIGHER LAW

When an English Lord remonstrated with Colonial Agent Franklin about the demonstrations and protests of Americans against British tax laws, Franklin recounted the action of a British vicar in the time of Charles II. The Merry Monarch had authorized the playing of games and sports on Sunday. A proclamation to that effect was ordered to be promulgated in every parish.

One rector who thought the writ violated the laws of Scripture posted on the church doors the regal writ. Under it he added, "This is the command of your king."

But beneath it he displayed the biblical injunction, "Remember to keep the Sabbath holy." And he added, "This is the Commandment of your God."

And finally he wrote, "Judge which of the two you should obey."

"HIS EYE IS ON THE SPARROW"

Shortly after the Constitutional Convention opened in 1787, the eighty-one-year-old Franklin pulled his feeble frame up to make a motion. When the presiding officer General Washington recognized him, Franklin, citing the language of Scripture, said, "If no sparrow can fall from the sky without His notice, surely no nation can rise from the ground without His help.

"I, therefore, move that we open the session by invoking His help with prayer."

A HOLE IN THE ARGUMENT

Franklin's plan for uniting the English colonies was called the Albany Union. His hopes for unity during the French threat from Canada were dashed by colonial leaders. They raised objections about central governmental control and cost.

Franklin said their arguments were contrived at the last minute. It reminded him of the boy who said on Sunday morning that he couldn't go to church because his shoes had holes in them—when he never mentioned the holes during the week.

HONEY AND VINEGAR

Because his almanac dispensed marital advice and advice to the lovelorn, Franklin was a forerunner of the advice columnists of today.

A young friend came to Franklin's house one day seeking counsel on a woman he was thinking of marrying. The besotted lad told Franklin, "I think she's perfect—but as you've said, 'Love is blind.'"

"How can I," continued the suitor, "find if she has any faults?"

Franklin offered this advice: "Talk to her girlfriends and praise her to the skies."

HORSE SENSE

As postmaster for the colonies, Franklin wore out many horses in his travels up and down the East Coast. In Providence, Rhode Island, he purchased a splendid equine specimen called a Narragansett Bay. Franklin was riding along Beacon Street in Boston when the mare, contrary to Franklin's commands, turned into the walkway to one house and stopped. To no avail, Franklin tried to make the horse move.

Finally, Franklin alit from the horse and knocked at the door of the house. When the owner appeared, Franklin said, "Sir, I am Benjamin Franklin from Philadelphia. I have no business with you; however, my horse has. She insists on coming to your house."

"Yes," the owner said with a laugh, "I recognize her. Her former owner was a friend of mine and used to visit me often."

Because of the horse, Franklin had a house to stay in that night!

HOT ROD

The British Stamp Act required that stamps be affixed to every product imported by the American colonists. In addition, the revenue-raising stamps were required not only for legal documents in the colonies, but also edicts and proclamations issued by the British government to be distributed to the American colonists.

Franklin, as agent for the colonies in London, thought this was adding insult to injury. When a British minister suggested that the stamp document was necessary for defraying the costs for issuing and transmitting the edict from London, Franklin said it reminded him of the Parisian who waited at the Seine River to accost British tourists.

Brandishing a hot poker, he asked, "Let me stick it up your ass?" When the startled Englishman exclaimed in the negative, the Frenchman then asked, "Well, then you should pay me for the expense of heating the poker."

"I CAN GET IT FOR YOU, WHOLESALE"

At age six, young Ben was regularly sent to the cellar by his father to tap a keg of ale to fill the glasses for the evening supper. When Franklin returned with a tray of brimming mugs, Josiah

Franklin—seated at the head of the family table—would then ask for God's blessing on the ale.

One night after the grace was delivered, the young Franklin asked, "Papa—when the ale arrives at the house—wouldn't it save the time of giving a blessing each night to bless the whole keg?"

IDLING IN NEUTRAL

For U.S. Minister Benjamin Franklin, it was a tall task of diplomacy to shake the policy of King Louis's France from neutrality into one of active support for the colonies in their War for Independence. King Louis hated England but was reluctant to assist an effort to topple a fellow monarch. At a formal state dinner, King Louis said, "Dr. Franklin, our chef has gone to great length to prepare this chicken recipe—his pièce de résistance—will you try his roast capon?"

"No," replied Franklin, thinking that a capon is a "neutered" chicken, "I decline to have anything to do with animals who are neutralized."

IT DOESN'T RING A BELL

Four years before his death, Benjamin Franklin received a Massachusetts town council. The town wished to rename itself Franklin after the Massachusetts native who had become the world's most revered statesman. In their letter the council proclaimed its plan to erect a bell tower for him.

Franklin wrote back that he was honored by the decision to name their town after him. But he said he wished the money that would be spent for the tower and the bell be used instead for the establishment of a library. Said Franklin, "I prefer books to bells and sense to sound."

"JOINT" EFFORT

When the Constitutional Convention deadlocked on the issue of representation, Franklin saw that some compromise had to be worked out. So he supported a two-house Congress with a House of Representatives elected on the basis of population and a Senate comprised of two from each state.

In his argument he referred to work in carpentry.

"When a broad table is to be made and the edges of planks do not fit, the artist takes a little from both and makes a good joint. In like manner, here both sides must part with some of their demands in order that they may join in some accommodating proposition."

LADIES FIRST

While Franklin was in London arguing the American cause, his seatmate one night at a banquet was an English countess. The lady, who had weathered a difficult marriage, flirted with Franklin as she chided him for his seditious views.

"Dr. Franklin," she asked, "why are you such a rebel?"

Franklin retorted, "Ma'am, it is tyranny that causes rebellion, and wives like you should be the first to recognize the chains of tyranny."

"LESS THAN MEETS THE EYE"

The most grievous ordeal of Franklin's life was the "Cockpit Trial" of 1774. Alexander Wedderburn, the attorney general for quite George III, was determined to jail Franklin for sedition and treason.

In a proceeding that smacked more of the Spanish Inquisition than a legal proceeding, this Scottish sycophant of King George arranged a star-chamber interrogation of the Pennsylvania agent. If Franklin murmured one response to his charges, Wedderburn would ask the court to jail him for contempt. For three hours, Wedderburn railed against Franklin—accusing him not only of fomenting rebellion, but of taking bribes from Philadelphia merchants—not to mention Franklin's being an adulterer and bastardizer. Franklin's only response was a cool grin.

When he provoked no reaction, Wedderburn's voice rose to a shrill rant as he screamed, "Franklin, you are less than a traitor, you're just a common fornicator and thief."

Franklin still voiced no response but his stoic smile.

When the proceeding was finished, Franklin made sure he ran into Wedderburn in the corridors of Whitehall.

Franklin said, "Wedderburn, anyone who strikes at a man who can't strike back is *less* than a man. And when America does strike back, you will find that you'll be serving a *lesser* king who has dominion over a *lesser* empire."

"LET GEORGE DO IT!"

In Paris, during the peace negotiations concluding the War for Independence, the freed American colonies were still not treated like a nation. There was even one banquet to which no American diplomats were invited.

The English ambassador and the French minister each offered a toast.

The French minister began: "To His Majesty, Louis the XVI, who, like the sun, fills the earth with a soft, benevolent glow."

The English ambassador followed with: "To George III, who, like the moon, spreads his light and illuminates the world."

Then Franklin barged into the banquet, making his way to the head table and raising his glass: "To General George Washington, the Joshua, who stopped the sun and moon in their tracks."

LIE-ING IN STATE?

When the Declaration of Independence was signed, the president of the congress, John Hancock, called Benjamin Franklin aside.

Said Hancock, "We have an important assignment for you."

Franklin rejoined, "I'm too old to be a soldier."

"No," answered Hancock, "we want you to be our minister to France."

"That's all right," quipped Franklin. "A soldier has to die for his country, but a diplomat only has to lie for his country."

LIGHT UP!

In 1774 Colonial Agent Franklin had become pessimistic about changing Parliament's oppressive tax policies. As storm clouds of approaching hostilities between England and the colonies darkened the skies, Franklin wrote from London to Charles Thomson, the secretary of the Continental Congress in Philadelphia.

"The sun of liberty is setting—it is time to light the candles of enterprise and economy."

THE LONG AND SHORT OF IT

One evening Franklin brought to a dinner in a French home a group of young American visitors to Paris.

A distinguished guest at the banquet was a venerable French academician from an old and noble family. As the evening wore into night and wine bottles were emptied, the scholar launched into his pet obsession—the New World, whose animals as well as human inhabitants manifested degenerate tendencies in both mind and body.

Franklin then asked all the Frenchmen to stand on one side of the table and all the Americans at the other side. The Americans in size and stature dwarfed their French counterparts.

"*Monsieur le Docteur,*" asked Franklin, "who is the tall and who the small? Who the hale, and who the frail?"

MAIDENLY PRESERVE

To build readership for his newspaper the Pennsylvania *Gazette,* Franklin sometimes concocted news items that would titillate even the "inquiring minds" who might read the supermarket tabloids of today.

One item he planted:

WILTSHIRE ENGLAND. A man aged 66 was married to a maid of 26—the match being made . . . on Wednesday . . . they were married on Thursday and the man died . . . on Friday. So that the bride was courted, married, became a wife, widow and we presume left a maiden all within 24 hours.

The contrived news item was a Franklin innovation.

MIND-SET

Franklin was reared a Presbyterian. In fact, it was his father's hope that Ben would become a Presbyterian minister. Franklin soon outgrew the rigid tenets of Calvinism for a stripped-down credo that stressed good deeds over theological doctrines, but he still attended the First Presbyterian Church in Philadelphia.

The minister, questioning his famous church attendant, heard Franklin describe his deistic beliefs.

"But, Dr. Franklin," the minister charged, "that's not orthodox."

Responded Franklin, "Orthodoxy is *my* doxy; heterodoxy is *your* doxy!"

MOTHER KNOWS LESS

In 1748 Franklin returned to Boston. The forty-two-year-old printer had not seen his native city since 1724, when he came back after a couple of years in Philadelphia.

One night before Franklin left, he discussed the topic of a mother's instinct in his Junto Club. Some members maintained that a mother could always recognize her own child. Franklin had doubts.

Franklin always used his own body and mind as a continuing laboratory. But this time he would use his mother as a guinea pig. He arrived in Boston at his old homestead handsomely clad, with his brown hair trimmed, and asked his mother if she had any rooms for lodgers. His mother bristled.

"What kind of woman do you think I am? I am no alewife. Perhaps on occasion I do put up some distinguished members of the Massachusetts General Assembly, but this is no common boardinghouse."

Franklin countered, "Well, that fire looks so inviting. Could I just sit for a while and warm myself?"

Mrs. Franklin nodded grudging assent and went on with her household tasks while her son proceeded to regale some overnight guests as well as some nephews who did not recognize him.

When afternoon turned to evening, she came back to warn her unwanted guest that if he wanted a room, he had better make inquiries while there was still time. Franklin, however, blithely continued his story-spinning to his appreciative audience. Soon it was nightfall and too late to find lodging. He then asked his annoyed mother if she could please give him a room. At the urging of the other guests, she allowed that he could sleep downstairs on the floor and she asked her black servant to keep an eye on the stranger.

The next morning after her guests informed her that the stranger was an educated man who spoke brilliantly on science, politics, and literature, she approached him and said, "What is your name?"

"Neb," Franklin replied. "Neb Frank."

"Where are you from?" she asked.

"Philadelphia," he replied.

"Perhaps then you know my son, Benjamin Franklin, the printer."

"As a matter of fact, I live in the same house with him. I know him quite well," and Franklin told her of his current accomplishments.

Then she said, "Neb, what kind of name is that? Is it short for Nebuchadrezzar?" Then it dawned on her. "Why, 'Neb' is backward for Ben," she said. "What kind of trick, Benjamin, have you played on your poor old mother?"

NO FREEBIES

Franklin's primary mission in his role as U.S. minister to France was to persuade King Louis XVI and his French government to abandon their policy of neutrality and adopt one in support of the American cause.

At a banquet of the royal court at Versailles, Franklin found himself seated next to a French count.

The nobleman turned to Franklin and said, "It is a grand game you are playing in the colonies with the British. What a spectacle you are offering!"

"Yes," said Franklin, "but the spectators are not paying."

NO PUSHOVER

In London, as the representative for Pennsylvania, Franklin argued to members of Parliament that their intransigence on the taxation problem was pushing the American colonies to war.

He said to one lord, "When you say that if we will just accept this latest tax, it would end the difficulties, it reminds me of an English colonel I knew some years ago who was negotiating with an Indian tribe.

"The chief invited the colonel to sit down with him on the log. When the colonel did, the chief asked him to move farther down. After the officer moved, the chief signaled him to slide farther down and again the officer repositioned himself.

"Then the chief gestured for him to move even farther down and the colonel said, 'But there's no more room. I'll fall off the log.'

"And the chief replied, 'That's what you've done to us—you've pushed us to the sea with your treaties. We can go no farther and we have to fight.'"

Summarized Franklin, "Sir, we can be pushed no farther!"

NOTHING DOING!

When the great William Pitt was dismissed by George III after the defeat of the French in the Seven Years War, the Tory prime minister who followed him was the feckless Lord Grenville, along with his ministry.

Their leadership, or lack of it, was a cause for concern for Colonial Agent Franklin. To a member of Parliament, Franklin said it reminded him of a ship where two sailors sneaked up from the deck to the helm.

A boatswain who caught sight of the two called up from the quarterdeck and asked, "Tom, what are you doing there?"

The abashed seaman said, "Nothing."

"And what are you doing, Jack?" he asked the man's companion.

"Helping him," was his reply.

"OH, YOU BEAUTIFUL DOLL . . ."

While Franklin was envoy to France, a collectible rage was a miniature Franklin with the head made of porcelain, with balding gray hair, and clad in his American long jacket and breeches.

One young fan invited Franklin to her boudoir to see her set of "little Franklins, all different in size and costume."

A beaming Franklin punned, "I have been i-doll-ized."

OLDEST PROFESSION?

In the 1780s, the new United States was floundering, with tariffs between the states bigger than those between European countries, and salaries for the national post office workers often suspended. One day during this period, Franklin entertained Dr. Benjamin Rush and Thomas Jefferson. The conversation turned to trying to determine what was the oldest profession.

Dr. Rush, a physician, said the oldest profession was his. "You see, it was a surgical operation that made Eve out of Adam's rib."

But Jefferson, who built Monticello, said, "No, it was the architect. After all, it was an architect who brought the world out of chaos."

Then replied Franklin, "You're both wrong. It's the politician. After all, who do you think created the chaos?"

"ONLY JUST BEGUN"

After the defeat of Cornwallis at Yorktown in 1781, a friend said to Franklin, "It looks as if the battle for independence is finally over."

Replied Franklin, "Sir, you are mistaken. The Revolutionary War may be over, but the battle for independence has just begun."

"OUT OF THE MOUTHS OF FOOLS . . ."

When Franklin arrived in Philadelphia as a young man, he left Puritan Boston and its Calvinist doctrines behind. Although he remained nominally a Presbyterian, he never concealed his disdain for the Puritan theologians and, for that matter, any theologians.

In his deistic beliefs, religious dogma was an anathema. Franklin thought preachers should urge good deeds—praising the heroes in daily life instead of damning the heretics.

Reportedly Franklin told the story of a Boston theologian who for years had traveled the circuit in New England. His sermon described in detail the agonies in hellfire that awaited those who defied God's doctrines.

As the preacher grew old, he hired a driver who would take him around in a small carriage to the churches. One day his illiterate driver said, "Doctor, I've heard your sermon so often I bet I could give it." The minister accepted the challenge.

In the next church meeting, the preacher sat in the back row and watched his driver, clad in the preacher's robes, deliver convincingly the torments of the damned.

After it was over, a man rose to ask a question. "Reverend Doctor, could you just explain divine grace?"

From the pulpit came the reply, "Why, that question is so foolishly simple that even my illiterate driver can answer it."

PAPERBOY

Josiah Franklin had twelve children. As the most famous of his offspring, Benjamin Franklin was looked to as the head of the large clan. Accordingly, advice as well as money were sometimes sought from the benevolent kinsman.

One child of his cousin frequently dunned Franklin for loans. On one occasion the lad—after receiving $20—promised, "But I'll pay it back, cousin Ben. Just give me a piece of paper and I'll sign an I.O.U."

"What?" chided Franklin in mock anger. "First you borrow money, and then you want to borrow the paper that's to guarantee the payment!"

PERUKE REBUKE

As the new minister of the American states to France, Benjamin Franklin had to present his credentials to King Louis XVI at his court at Versailles.

When it was heard that Franklin was not in the habit of wearing a wig, a courtier advised Franklin to outfit himself with one.

Franklin demurred, saying, "What matters is what you have inside your head—not on top of it."

PLAINCLOTHES MAN

It is told that when Franklin was packing to sail to France to be U.S. minister, his daughter Sally urged him to have new clothes made that would be fit for his diplomatic services in Versailles in the court of Louis XVI.

"Papa," she said, "you must look the part of an ambassador."

Replied Franklin, "I'll look the part of an American—not like a prince, but a pioneer."

PRACTICAL POLITICS

While visiting David Hume in Edinburgh, Franklin heard from the Scottish philosopher a discourse in metaphysics.

Franklin listened and then said, "David, I understand its theoretical value, but what is its practical value?"

Answered Hume, "I don't know—how do you measure practical value?"

Franklin replied with a chuckle, "Anything the British Parliament would like to tax."

PRESSING DEMAND

As a young printer in Philadelphia, Franklin was anxious to leave the employ of William Keimer and set up a shop of his own. Yet Franklin knew he needed some competitive edge. After all, he was not a native of Philadelphia and could not count on referrals from any family connection.

Franklin knew that Governor Keith of Pennsylvania had the habit of taking his supper at the City Tavern. One afternoon after Keith was enjoying his postprandial Madeira wine, the twenty-eight-year old Franklin went up to the governor and said, "Your Excellency, you are the governor of Pennsylvania and Philadelphia—the second largest city in the empire of King George II—and the manifestos, proclamations, as well as the statutes of this Commonwealth should carry a printing style that befits such eminence."

The royal governor was bemused by the young man's suggestion, so Franklin broached his idea.

"I am a printer, Governor Keith, and I would suggest you send me to London to buy the latest printing presses."

Keith agreed and dispatched Franklin to London. Franklin did study the modern techniques of the day, but Keith reneged and did not send him money for return. Said Franklin later, "It was the last time I trusted a politician."

"PRINCIPAL" CONCERN

Like the farmers he published the almanac for, Franklin was both economical in his habits and earthy in his humor.

Once, in preaching thrift to a nephew, he recounted the tale of a Quaker gentleman in Philadelphia who had caught his young son in his bedroom indulging in autoerotic pursuits.

The father, in remonstrating with the boy, reminded him of a Quaker tenet and cited, "Thee must not play with the 'principal.'"

THE PROUD AND PROFANE

While the French were invading western Pennsylvania, Franklin tried to convince the Quakers of Philadelphia of the need to organize militia for defense.

One Quaker leader smiled placidly at Franklin's urgings. "We are pacifists. The Presbyterians aren't. Those Scotch-Irish hotheads will do enough fighting for both of us."

Franklin said that the man's attitude reminded him of another Quaker friend of his. He was a farmer who had problems with a stubborn mule.

Said the Quaker to his mule, "Thee knows I won't curse or swear at thee. But remember I can sell thee to the Anglican across the street who will."

RAIN-OUT

At a Junto meeting, the topic turned to the most pitiful sight each had ever seen. One spoke of a blind man, another of a lame wretch.

Franklin answered, "The sorriest sight is the lonely man on a rainy day who cannot read."

RAT FINK

In the 1750s, when the French in the Ohio Valley were knocking on Pennsylvania's door, Franklin set to work shoring up the defenses of the commonwealth. When one merchant balked at financial support of the newly organized Pennsylvania militia, he said, "Franklin, why should I help to save Quakers who won't fight to defend themselves?"

Replied Franklin, "You're like the sailor who won't caulk the leaky ship because it would save the rats."

RE-TURN-COAT

Franklin was one of the three U.S. commissioners appointed by the Continental Congress to negotiate the treaty following the War for Independence from Great Britain. Franklin could not forget his last encounter with ministers of the Crown eight years earlier when

Franklin, in star-chamber proceedings, was bullied by the British attorney general in a three-hour inquisition to force from him a guilty plea to sedition and treason.

At the formal signing ceremonies in Paris, his cocommissioner Silas Deane—himself clad in brocaded silks and velvet finery—chided Franklin for his sartorial selection of an old and tattered brown coat.

Replied Franklin, "I wore that jacket on that day of the Cockpit Trial prosecution by the English attorney general—and today I wanted to give that old brown coat a little revenge."

RICHES AND RAGS

In England in the 1760s Franklin visited one of the new clothing mills in Norwich. The manager showed him the factory, where oppressed workers—including children and women—toiled twelve hours a day at the spinning machines turning out woven cloth in scenes that would later inspire Charles Dickens's sympathy.

The superintendent bragged, "Dr. Franklin, we ship the cloth all over the world. To Paris, Madrid, Rome, and, yes, Boston and Philadelphia, where the best-dressed ladies and gentlemen wear our products."

Franklin, pointing to some ragged women pushing the looms, asked dryly, "Do you ship to Norwich?"

THE RIGHT FIGURE

When Franklin served as the colonies' representative in London, the king's prime minister, Lord Townshend, asked him to read over the proposed Stamp Act and comment on it. Franklin did and told the British minister that it was fine—if he would make one little change. Townshend was surprised that Franklin seemed so amenable and asked him what the correction was. "Oh," said Franklin, "just change the word *one* in the bill to *two*."

Townshend reread the bill to look for the change. When he found it he went to Franklin: "If we change to *two* the only *one* in the bill," Townshend exploded, "it would mean that the Stamp Act statute would become operative not in 1774 but 2774."

Replied Franklin, "You figure right."

RIGHT RITE?

While in London, Franklin, who abhorred theology, found himself once in the midst of a heated doctrinal altercation between a member of an old Catholic family and an Anglican bishop. Franklin said, "Your Grace, you Anglicans say you are never in the wrong, yet the Catholics proclaim they are infallible.

"The argument between you," offered Franklin, "reminds me of a beautiful woman whose argumentative nature discouraged marriage proposals. One frustrated suitor said, 'Why must you always contradict?' She replied, 'I don't know how it happens, but I meet with nobody except myself who is *always* in the right.'"

ROYAL FLUSH

In his sojourn as U.S. minister to France, Franklin found himself lionized by French hostesses. He was invited to dinners, dances, and sometimes to play chess. One chess companion was the Duchess of Bourbon, a relative of King Louis XVI.

As the table was being set up, Franklin took the two king pieces off the board. To the startled Duchess, Franklin flashed an impish smile and said, "In America, we have no need for kings."

SHOCK SOCK

During his experiments with electricity, Franklin wanted to test the electrocution of animals. For his test on a turkey, he invited a friend to observe the procedure. When Franklin administered the jolt of electricity, he mistakenly touched the wire attached to the turkey. Instead of the turkey, it was Franklin who was knocked out. When Franklin awoke close to a minute later, he looked up at his friend and whispered, "Instead of a dead turkey, it was almost a cooked goose!"

SHORT-"CHANGED"?

Franklin was an inveterate prankster. Before he left his first job as a printing apprentice to William Keimer in Philadelphia in 1723, he contrived a special typo.

For a reading primer, this hymn had been included:

When the last trumpet soundeth
We shall not all die
But we shall be changed
In the twinkling of an eye

Franklin shortened *changed* to *hanged* by eliminating the *c*. So it read:

But we shall be hanged
In the twinkling of an eye

SIGNPOSTS

The Continental Congress first asked Franklin, the colonies' most famous author, to write the Declaration of Independence. Franklin, who knew any draft that was proposed would undergo severe editing, demurred. He much preferred editing to being the edited. So he persuaded the thirty-two-year-old delegate from Virginia, Thomas Jefferson, to be the writer.

When Jefferson agreed, Franklin took the young Virginian out of his house on High Street and pointed down the block. "Do you see that sign with a picture of a hat? Well, originally it said JOHN THOMPSON, HATTER—MAKES AND SELLS HATS FOR READY CASH AND MONEY. Then friends told him the word 'Hatter' was redundant so he struck it off. Later they told him to eliminate 'make' since customers buying hats wouldn't care who made them.

"Then after a while a friend told Thompson to take out the words 'ready money and cash' because no one sold on credit.

"Finally it said, JOHN THOMPSON SELLS HATS. Still that was too long—so Thompson left only the picture of the hat.

"So, Jefferson," advised Franklin, "if you want to beat the editors, your words must be as spare as that sign."

SILENCE WAS GOLDEN!

Gouverneur Morris was a prominent delegate in the Constitutional Convention. He disdained those who addressed him by his Christian name and particularly took offense when they made it sound like "governor." Morris, who was insistent on the correct French pronunciation, would admit few Americans as his social peer.

One exception was George Washington. Morris confided to Franklin, "I'm one of the few who address General Washington as 'George.'"

On one morning when Franklin sighted George Washington approaching the State House on his horse, he nudged Morris and said, "Gouverneur Morris, here comes your friend George."

Washington alit from his horse and strode up the steps of the State House to hear Morris boom out, "Hello, George."

Washington drilled him with his blue eyes and strode silently past the chagrined Morris. Franklin had set up the pompous Morris for a fall in influence among his fellow delegates.

SLAVES MAKE WAVES

At the Constitutional Convention an argument arose between the northern and southern states on slaves as property. Thomas Lynch, a delegate from South Carolina, questioned the idea that slaves be taxed at a greater rate.

"Why," said Lynch, "should slaves be taxed more than sheep, for example?"

Franklin answered, "Slaves sap instead of strengthening the nation—and there is a big difference. Sheep will not rise up and rebel."

SNEEZY AND SNOOTY

Gouverneur Morris one day was sniffing and sneezing. "I feel sorry for him," said Franklin.

"Why?" said another delegate. "It's just the common cold."

"That's just it," said Franklin. "Poor Morris can't bear to think he has anything common about him."

SNOB RULE?

When Franklin was touting the virtues of the new American republic as minister to France, one French aristocrat challenged him.

"How do you like it, Franklin, being ruled by people you wouldn't have dinner with?"

Retorted Franklin, "Better than to be ruled by those who wouldn't invite you to their house for dinner."

SNOW WHITE

When the fifty-year-old Franklin was making his rounds as postmaster general, a buxom eighteen-year-old from Providence, Rhode Island, flirted with him.

Franklin, resisting any thought of dalliance, said, "Dear, you are like the snow—pure like your virginal innocence, white as your lovely bosom . . . and likely to be just as cold."

SPEED MERCHANT

Lord Sandwich was one of the principal advocates of the Crown's policy of taxation. In a Parliamentary gallery Franklin heard the Tory leader rant on about the ungrateful American colonists.

Franklin turned to a companion and remarked, "His tongue is just like one of those racing horses he breeds. The less weight it has, the faster it runs."

"SPIRITUAL" BLESSING

In the French and Indian War, Franklin—in his new role as general—marched militia forces up the Delaware River to Bethlehem to build a fort.

As the work erecting the barricades commenced, the troop chaplain, a Presbyterian minister named Beatty, complained that the soldiers were not attending the nightly prayer meeting in the fort.

"Parson," Franklin questioned Beatty, "do you drink?"

"No," replied the offended clergyman.

Franklin continued, "But you do serve it in communion?"

The minister nodded his assent.

"Well," said Franklin, "I will appoint you the official purveyor of the camp's allotment of rum and you will serve it directly after prayers."

Afterward the prayer sessions were never better attended.

SPIT IN THE OCEAN

In 1775 Franklin, the colonial agent in London, saw no chance of dissuading Britain from its punitive tax policy. As the storm clouds of war threatened, some colonials beseeched King George III for merciful intercession. A document called the Olive Branch Petition, with hundreds of signatures of leading American colonials, was brought to London.

An American representative of the delegation presented the petition to Franklin, saying, "If only King George could read this, he'd know our loyalty to His Majesty and he would stop Parliament from its oppressive taxation."

Franklin picked up the petition and waved it in the air, saying, "It's only a hiccup in a hurricane."

SQUEEZE PLAY

In Philadelphia, Benjamin Franklin's print shop was being threatened by the city Proprietors, who had decided that Franklin's opinions on freedom ought to be silenced. This elite of city fathers cut him out of all government contracts and legal documents in both city and province in the hope that this would drive him to bankruptcy. Franklin decided to send out engraved invitations to some of the Proprietors to come to his house. Out of curiosity, they came.

At each place was set a bowl of something that looked like dry, gray mush. Franklin, at the head of the table, took a pitcher of water, added some to his bowl, and then proceeded to wolf down the contents greedily.

One of the guests then poured some water into his bowl and tried a spoonful. He quickly spat it out, saying, "Franklin, what the devil is in this bowl?"

Franklin replied, "Plain old sawdust. And if you understand that I can live off that and like it, you ought to know that you'll never squeeze me out of my business."

STINKEROO!

When Franklin was Pennsylvania's agent in London to lobby against the Crown's punitive tax legislation, he became the subject of vicious rumors. One British lord was spreading the canards that Franklin was a violator of contracts, a recipient of merchant bribes, and a seducer of innocent maidens. A friend of Franklin's suggested that he challenge the spreader of the rumors to a duel.

Franklin related the story of a business acquaintance who told a man with poor hygiene habits that he stank. When the insulted man challenged his critic to a duel, Franklin's acquaintance said, "If we had a duel and you won, you would still stink. But if I killed you, you would stink even more."

STOUT FELLOW

Benjamin Franklin was a little rotund in his later life and it was said that in Paris a young woman, tapping him on his protruding abdomen, said, "Dr. Franklin, if this were on a woman, we'd know what to think."

And Franklin replied, "Half an hour ago, mademoiselle, it was on a woman, and now what do you think?"

SUSPICION AND SEDITION

Franklin, as the colonial agent in London, was constantly bombarded by British ministers with exaggerated reports of American outbursts of dissent.

"Franklin," one minister charged, "we know that you Americans are secretly plotting rebellion."

"Sir," replied Franklin, "you remind me of the husband who—suspicious of his wife—constantly accused her of infidelity. Eventually his accusations drove her into an affair she had never contemplated until her husband had tempted her with the joy of such illicit bliss."

SWEET DREAMS

Women of all ages were attracted to Franklin's wit and charm. When one mademoiselle complained to Franklin that he hadn't paid a visit to her all summer, the gallant Franklin replied, "I was waiting until the nights were longer."

"TIME IS MONEY"

Franklin's printing shop in Philadelphia sold books. One day a man walked in and picked up a book. "How much is it?" he asked Franklin.

"Two shillings," was the reply.

The would-be purchaser demurred and haggled with Franklin over the cost. He then said to Franklin, "I'll give you only one shilling and sixpence."

Franklin replied, "The price is three shillings."

"What?" said the buyer. "You said earlier it was two shillings."

"The price is now three," said Franklin. "You have cost me in argument another shilling's worth of my time."

TWO HEADS AREN'T BETTER THAN ONE!

Among the weirder exhibits Franklin showcased in the mini-museum and laboratory he called his house was an embalmed two-headed snake. Franklin occasionally pointed out the herpetological monstrosity to dramatize his advocacy of a unicameral legislature instead of a two-house system, as existed in Britain and France and in all the colonies except Pennsylvania.

To delegates to the Constitutional Convention who dropped in to visit, Franklin would point out his two-headed snake and then tell how it died. "You see, one head wanted to go one way to the pond," said Franklin tongue-in-cheek, "but the other head argued the other way for the stream.

"The moral is," summed up Franklin, "the poor serpent died of thirst."

UNPOPULAR MECHANICS

In the 1750s the merchants of Philadelphia—reflecting their new status in wealth—organized a Philadelphia ball. The dance would be the occasion for their handsomely gowned daughters to meet the right young men. A few tradesmen who owned shops were admitted, but mechanics were barred.

Franklin sought out the chairman of the ball and said, "Would you exclude the Lord God Almighty?"

The merchant was taken aback. Then Franklin added, "After all, He is the greatest mechanic—doesn't the Scripture say, 'He makes all things by weight and measure'?"

"VANITY, SAITH THE PREACHER . . ."

Franklin was once the guest of a man who had spent most of his fortune to build a stately mansion.

Franklin observed on the fireplace a mantelpiece with the inscription *"Oia Vanitas."* Franklin, who disdained the use of dead languages such as Greek and Latin as affectation, asked his host what the words meant.

The owner said, "I had in mind a smooth marble mantlepiece for my fireplace. *'Omnia Vanitas'* [All is vanity] was what I chose to inscribe on it, but there was not room enough on the marble piece to fit and still have it legible—so I contracted it—after all, Latin mottoes are often contracted—shortening it to *'Oia Vanitas.'"*

Franklin said, "I understand the meaning of your motto—in the building of your house you had to abridge your *'omnia'* but you would not shorten your *'vanitas.'"*

A WHALE OF A JOB

During his tour in London as Pennsylvania's lobbyist to the British Parliament, Franklin found himself increasingly amused and even exasperated by the Englishmen's conceptions about life in America. To the Londoner, the colonies were one grand primeval forest full of exiled convicts and fierce redskins. No tale about America's physical splendor or moral squalor was too tall to be disbelieved.

At one dinner Franklin's English host mentioned the Niagara Falls and asked if Franklin had seen them.

"Yes," and Franklin added with a straight face, "it's quite a sight to see the killer whales shooting up the falls."

WIFE AFTER DEATH?

In the 1740s Franklin was among a group boarding a ship from Philadelphia to New York. To get to the boat, passengers—twelve at a time—would take a canoe. The canoe overturned in the Delaware River. All were picked up safely. When they arrived in New York, Franklin treated his fellow canoe riders to a round of drinks at a New York tavern.

One of his former ferrymates bragged of helping save the life of the famous Franklin. Franklin, who was a superb swimmer, genially let the boast pass unchallenged.

But in the years that followed, the self-anointed savior milked this claim to dun Franklin for some "loans." Franklin, against his better judgment, would give something, and over the years it mounted to a considerable sum.

The old cadger eventually died. Yet to Franklin's consternation he received a letter from the widow asking for more financial aid.

Franklin explained to his wife, "He seems to have left me his wife as part of her dowry."

THE WORLD'S MY OYSTER

When Benjamin Franklin was the British postmaster general of the colonies, he had to visit the major cities of all the thirteen Colonies to set up post offices.

A weary Franklin used to arrive at an inn after a long day's horseback ride to find all the chairs by the warming hearth taken.

So one day when he pulled into Hartford at seven in the evening, Franklin announced to the innkeeper, "A bucket of oysters for my horse." When the host expressed astonishment, Franklin repeated his instructions, and all the inn's guests vacated their seats close to the fire to witness this extraordinary equine who ate oysters. Franklin then took a choice seat by the fireplace.

Minutes later, the innkeeper, with a throng of guests, rushed back into the inn.

"Franklin," they exclaimed, "your horse won't eat the oysters!"

"In that case," replied Franklin from his seat by the fire, "give me the oysters and give my horse some hay!"

"WRITE" WAY—WRONG WAY

While Franklin was at the court at Versailles negotiating for the loan from King Louis XVI that would keep George Washington's Continental Army in the field, his friend John Paul Jones was in Le Havre writing letters to the French king to ask him for some warships. Yet Jones sent letter after letter to no avail.

When the recognition treaty with France and the loan to the Continental Congress were finally signed, Franklin, with his mission completed, prepared to sail back to Philadelphia.

Upon embarking from port at Le Havre, Franklin left a package for Jones. It was a personally inscribed book that had translated his sayings of Poor Richard into French. A book marker led Jones to one adage:

"If you would have your business done, go—if not—send."

Jones took Franklin's advice. He journeyed to Versailles to see King Louis, who answered his request by outfitting him with three ships. Captain John Paul Jones named his flagship *Le Bonhomme Richard* ("Poor Richard," in French). It was on that ship fighting the British man-o'-war, the *Serapis,* that Jones would coin the most ringing catchphrase of the war: "I have not yet begun to fight."

Valedictory

At the close of the Constitutional Convention, Franklin, the oldest delegate of the assembly, was invited to be the first to sign the document. The feeble Franklin—using the benches as support—propelled himself to the front table in the State House forum at which the presiding officer sat.

Looking at the chair from which George Washington had presided in the convention sessions, Franklin noted that the chair's back featured a design of a sun low on the horizon, its rays extending into the sky.

Franklin said, "I have often observed the picture on this chair of a sun low on the horizon and I confess that there were days in this convention that I thought it was a picture of a setting sun. But today I know it was a design of a rising sun. A new dawn of freedom and a new day for America."

Benediction

As news spread in Philadelphia that the Constitutional Convention was concluding its business in September 1787, citizens gathered outside the old State House to hear what had happened.

The first face to appear when the white double doors of the hall opened was that of Benjamin Franklin. Cheers then greeted Philadelphia's most famous citizen.

Then a middle-aged lady named Mrs. Powell yelled from the back, "Dr. Franklin, what kind of government did you give us? A monarchy or a republic?"

Franklin shot back, "A republic—if you can keep it!"

Postscript

In 1790 a dying Benjamin Franklin lay in his bed attended by his daughter, Sara Franklin Bache. A knock on the door announced a visitor bringing a letter from the President's house.

A half-blind Franklin said, "Sally, please read it to me."

She read aloud President Washington's words, which ended:

If to be venerated for benevolence, if to be admired for talents, if to be esteemed for patriotism, if to be beloved for philanthropy, can gratify the human mind, you have the pleasing consolation to know that you have not lived in vain.

Epitaph

Franklin at the young age of twenty-one wrote his epitaph. Though it would be amended over the years, the final version reads:

The Body of
B. Franklin
Printer

Like the cover of an old book,
Its contents turned out
and stripped of its lettering and gilding
Lies here, food for worms
But the work shall not be wholly lost;
For it will, as he believed, appear once more,
In a new more perfect edition
Corrected and amended
By the Author.

Ben's Time Line

HIS LIFE	YEAR	HIS WORLD
Born January 17 in Boston, the son of Josiah Franklin and Abiah Folger	1706	John Churchill, the Duke of Marlborough, defeats the French and conquers the Spanish Netherlands
Printing apprentice to brother James in Boston	1718	Voltaire at age twenty-four is imprisoned at the Bastille; William Penn dies in England
Silence Dogood essays published anonymously by New England *Courant*	1722	Peter the Great defeats Persia to gain control of the Caspian Sea
Runs away to Philadelphia	1723	John Sebastian Bach composes *St. John's Passion*
Sails to London to study latest innovations in printing	1724	Treaty of Stockholm between Peter the Great's Russia and Sweden
Returns to Philadelphia and sets up printing shop	1726	Spain conquers and settles Uruguay
Establishes newspaper the Pennsylvania *Gazette*	1727	Isaac Newton dies, George II is crowned

HIS LIFE	YEAR	HIS WORLD
Becomes sole owner of the Pennsylvania *Gazette*	1730	John and Charles Wesley found Methodism
Establishes first circulating library in America	1731	Pragmatic Sanction (Treaty of Britain, Holland, Spain to guarantee Austria)
Publishes his almanac	1732	Alexander Pope writes *Essays of Man*
Appointed clerk of Pennsylvania General Assembly	1736	Russia and Austria attack Turkey
Appointed postmaster of Philadelphia	1737	Spain conquers Naples and Sicily—installs Don Carlos as king of the Two Sicilies
Invents Franklin stove	1742	Handel's *Messiah* first performed; Sir Robert Walpole forced to resign as British prime minister
Makes kite test of lightning and electricity	1747	Samuel Johnson publishes his dictionary
Elected to the Philadelphia Common Council—retires from printing—turns it over to shop foreman	1748	Montesquieu writes *Spirit of the Law*
Grand master, Pennsylvania Masons	1749	Georgia becomes Crown colony; Tobias Smollett publishes novel *Roderick Random*
Charters Pennsylvania Hospital	1751	Clive defeats French in India; Diderot publishes *Encyclopedia*; Thomas Gray writes *Elegy Written in a Country Churchyard*

HIS LIFE	YEAR	HIS WORLD
Establishes first American fire insurance company; invents lightning conductor	1752	Britain adopts Gregorian calendar
Receives honorary degrees from Harvard and Yale	1753	Parliament establishes British Museum; George Washington makes expedition to Ohio to scout French inroads
Colonies reject Franklin's Albany Union Confederation plan	1754	Chippendale produces famous work on furniture
Elected to the Royal Society	1756	Black Hole of Calcutta; Mozart is born in Salzburg
Goes to London as agent for Pennsylvania	1757	William Pitt becomes prime minister, leads war against France
Receives honorary degree from St. Andrew's University in Scotland	1759	Josiah Wedgwood builds his ceramic factory
Receives honorary degree from Oxford	1762	Oliver Goldsmith publishes *Vicar of Wakefield*; Rousseau writes *Social Contract*
Defeated for reelection to General Assembly by pro-Proprietor faction	1764	James Hargreaves invents spinning jenny; Mozart begins tour as child prodigy
Back in London as colonial agent, works for repeal of Stamp Act	1765	Sir William Blackstone publishes his commentaries on the law of England
Elected president of the American Philosophical Society; becomes colonial agent in London for New Jersey as well as Pennsylvania	1769	Captain James Cook explores east coast of Australia; Goethe publishes first poems; Sir Joshua Reynolds first president of the Royal Academy
Campaigns against Townshend Duties	1770	Gainsborough paints *Blueboy*
Amends and publishes *Autobiography*	1771	Russia conquers Crimea; destroys Turkish fleet

HIS LIFE	YEAR	HIS WORLD
Elected to French Academy of Sciences	1772	Joseph Priestley discovers oxygen
"Cockpit Trial"; Intolerable tax acts passed by Parliament	1774	Edmund Burke writes *American Taxation*
Returns to America; elected to Continental Congress; becomes postmaster general again	1775	James Watt manufactures steam engine; Catherine the Great reorganizes Russia—centralizes control
Serves on review committee for Declaration of Independence—swings Pennsylvania to side of patriot cause	1776	Adam Smith writes *Wealth of Nations*
Negotiates treaty with France	1778	William Pitt, Earl of Chatham, dies; Sheridan stages *The School for Scandal*
Becomes Governor of Pennsylvania	1779	David Garrick, Britain's most famous actor, dies
Franklin returns to France	1781	Immanuel Kant writes *Critique of Reason*
Signs Treaty of Versailles—observes balloon flights	1782	Irish Parliament made independent of Great Britain
Elected delegate to U.S. Constitutional Convention—becomes president (governor) of Pennsylvania	1785	Russians settle Aleutians; Alexander Cartwright patents his power loom
Concludes work at Constitutional Convention	1787	King Louis XVI convokes Assembly of Notables to consider taxation of lords
Finishes last section of *Autobiography*—submits memorial to U.S. Congress to ban slavery	1789	Storming of Bastille—French Revolution begins—Jeremy Bentham publishes his economic philosophy
April 17, Franklin dies at age eighty-four	1790	Robert Burns writes "Tam O'Shanter"; Mozart writes *Così Fan Tutti*

Bibliography

Aldridge, Alfred Owen. *Benjamin Franklin*. Philadelphia: Lippincott, 1965.

Bigelow, John, ed. *The Autobiography of Benjamin Franklin*. Philadelphia: Lippincott, 1868.

Block, Seymour Stanton. *Benjamin Franklin: His Wit and Wisdom*. New York: Hastings House, 1975.

Bowen, Catherine Drinker. *The Most Dangerous Man in America*. Boston: Little, Brown, 1974.

Clark, Ronald W. *Benjamin Franklin*. New York: Random House, 1983.

Crane, Verner W., ed. *Benjamin Franklin's Letters to the Press*. Chapel Hill: University of North Carolina Press, 1950.

Ford, Paul. *The Many Sided Franklin*. New York: Century, 1899.

Franklin, Benjamin, and D. Hall. *Poor Richard's Almanac*. Philadelphia, 1733–1758.

Hale, Edward E., ed. *Franklin in France* (vols. 1–2). Boston: Roberts Brothers, 1888.

Jordan, Helen and Clarence, eds. *Benjamin Franklin's Unfinished Business*. Philadelphia: Franklin Institute, 1956.

Keyes, Nelson. *Ben Franklin*. Garden City, NY: Hanover House, 1956.

Labaree, Leonard, ed. *The Papers of Benjamin Franklin* (vols. 1–18). New Haven: Yale University Press, 1978.

Labaree, Leonard, and Whitfield Bell, Jr., eds. *Mr. Franklin*. New Haven: Yale University Press, 1956.

Lokken, Roy N. *Meet Dr. Franklin.* Philadelphia: Franklin Institute, 1981.

Lopez, Claudia-Anne, and Eugenia W. Herbert. *The Private Franklin.* New York: Norton, 1975.

Meadowcraft, Enid LaMonte. *Benjamin Franklin.* New York: Crowell, 1941.

Morris, Charles. *Admiral Franklin? Yes, Admiral Franklin.* New York: Privately printed, 1975.

Morris, Charles, ed. *America's Big Ben.* New York: Privately printed, 1963.

Morris, Charles, ed. *Franklin Was There.* New York: Privately printed, 1962.

Nolan, J. Bennett. *Benjamin Franklin in Scotland and Ireland.* Philadelphia: University of Pennsylvania Press, 1938.

Randall, Willard. *A Little Revenge.* Boston: Little, Brown, 1984.

Russell, Phillips. *Benjamin Franklin: First Civilized American.* New York: Brentano's, 1926.

Thayer, W. M. *From Boyhood to Manhood: The Life of Franklin.* New York: Hurst, 1889.

Van Doren, Carl. *Benjamin Franklin.* New York: Viking, 1938.

Van Doren, Carl, ed. *Benjamin Franklin's Autobiographical Writings.* New York: Viking, 1945.

Weems, Mason L. *The Life of Benjamin Franklin.* Baltimore: 1815.

Wright, Esmond. *Franklin of Philadelphia.* Cambridge, MA: Harvard University Press, 1986.

Index